Arthur
Makes the Team

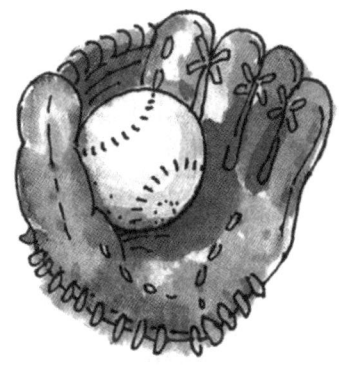

For Tucker

Chapter 1

Buster and Arthur were walking along the **sidewalk** with their baseball **glove**s. As they walked, they **toss**ed a ball **back and forth**.

"So, do you think you'll be good at baseball?" Buster asked.

Arthur **shrug**ged. "I hope so," he said. He didn't want to **admit** to being **nervous**. He hadn't played last year, like some of the other kids.

"Did you learn a lot last year?" he asked.

Buster laughed. "Did I? Let me show you. Run out for a long catch."

Arthur **trot**ted past a tree.

Buster **wave**d him on. "**Farther** . . . farther . . . Okay, stand there. Are you ready? See if you can catch the famous Buster Ball."

"Ready!" said Arthur. He held up his glove.

Buster threw the ball as hard as he could. But instead of going toward Arthur, the ball **shot** up into a tree. It **bounce**d around in the **branch**es.

"I've got it," said Arthur, circling **underneath**.

The ball bounced down off one branch, then another, before rolling onto a **roof**.

"I've still got it," said Arthur, **follow**ing the ball's every move.

The ball rolled down the roof and into the **gutter**. It shot out the **bottom** of the **downspout**, passed between Arthur's legs, and rolled into a storm **drain**.

"Oops!" said Arthur. "I guess I don't have it **after all**."

Buster looked down the drain. He **sigh**ed. "I lose more balls that way."

"That was a pretty **amazing** throw," said Arthur. "And you learned that in just one season?"

"I sure did. Don't worry—you'll **catch on** quickly. Just think: you're standing out there in the middle of the **field**. There's no one around."

"No one around," said Arthur.

"No place to hide," said Buster.

"No place to hide," Arthur **repeat**ed.

"At the **crack** of the **bat**, the ball is headed your way. Everyone is **staring**, watching your every move."

"My every move?" said Arthur.

"Of course," said Buster. "And not just your team**mate**s. The other team is watching, too. And the **crowd** in the **stand**s. **Especially** your family."

"My family?"

Buster **nod**ded. "Sure. Parents. Grandparents. Sisters. Everybody comes to the games."

Arthur sighed. "Let me **get** this **straight**. I'm all alone in the middle of the field, and the whole world is watching whenever the ball comes to me."

"Pretty **exciting**, huh?" said Buster.

"I guess," said Arthur. *Exciting* wasn't actually the word he had in mind.

"And don't forget batting," said Buster.

"No, I wouldn't want to do that."

Buster **crouch**ed down in a batting **stance**. "It's just you and the **pitcher**. Nothing else **matters**. You **raise** your bat. Ready. Waiting. The **pitch blaze**s in. You can feel the heat as the ball passes by."

Arthur **swallow**ed. "You feel the heat?"

"Well, maybe not," Buster admitted. "But it's a **tense** moment."

"Because everyone is watching."

"**Exact**ly. The **umpire** calls, 'Strike!' But that's okay. It wasn't your pitch. But now you stand in."

"Stand in," said Arthur.

"It's another fastball. But this time you **swing**. The ball **streak**s like a rocket. It's a home run! You circle the **base**s to the **cheer**s of the crowd."

"**Just like that**?" said Arthur.

"Well, not every time. But it could happen if you're lucky."

Arthur sighed. He didn't know if that would happen to him. But it was nice to think about.

Chapter

2

At the ball **field**, a **bunch** of kids were **huddle**d around the **bulletin board**, looking at the team **roster**s.

"I found my name," said Buster. "Let's see . . . Francine . . . Brain . . . Binky . . . Arthur. Yes! Yes! We're all on the Eagles together. Hey, this is going to be a great team. I can't wait to start **pitch**ing."

"Hey, I want to pitch!" said Francine.

"So do I," said the Brain.

"How will we **choose**?" asked Buster.

"Don't worry," said Francine. "The **coach**

will **decide**."

"But Francine," said the Brain, "your father is the coach."

She smiled. "Funny how these things **work out**."

"How what things work out?" asked her father, coming up to join them. He **had on** his **official** Eagles hat and T-shirt.

"Nothing, Daddy," said Francine, smiling at him.

"I think I'm going to be sick," **whisper**ed Buster.

"I think you'll have **company**," the Brain whispered back.

The whole team—**including** Sue Ellen, Speedy, Fern, and Alex—sat down in the **grass**.

"I'm glad everyone could be here for our first **practice**," said the coach. "As most of you know, I'm Oliver Frensky, Francine's dad."

Francine gave Buster a big smile.

"Now, our **motto** is going to be 'Teamwork!'" the coach went on. "If you have a favorite **position**, you can start with that. But you'll all be moving around. Who's going to be our first **pitcher**?"

Buster, Francine, and the Brain all **raise**d their hands.

"Excellent. We have a whole **staff**. Buster, why don't you go first?"

"But . . . but—," Francine **sputter**ed.

"You'll get your **turn**," her father **reassure**d her.

Everyone else took a position. Arthur **end**ed **up** in right field. Nobody else seemed to want to be there.

"Heads up, everyone!" said the coach, waiting with a **bat** at home plate.* "Go ahead,

---

★**home plate** [야구 용어] 홈 플레이트. 본루. 주자가 득점하기 위해서 밟아야 하는 오각형 모양의 베이스.

13

Buster."

Buster **prepare**d to pitch. He **twirl**ed his arm around, **shot** out his leg, and threw as hard as he could.

Coach Frensky **blink**ed.

"Where did the ball go?"

Buster wasn't sure. He was never sure with a Buster Ball. A moment later the ball came down and hit him on the head.

"Are you all right, Buster?" asked the coach.

Buster **nod**ded.

"Good. Try again. But this time **ease** up a little. Don't **wear** your arm out the first day."

Buster nodded. He pitched again—and the ball **sail**ed right over the plate. The coach lined a drive★ to Sue Ellen at third **base**.

After a few more pitches, it was Francine's

★ **line a drive** 라인 드라이브를 치다. 라인 드라이브는 공을 타격하여 거의 일직선으로 날아가게 하는 것을 말한다.

turn. Her first pitches were high and outside. Her father **foul**ed them off.

"Nice energy," he said. "Remember now, right over the plate."

Francine's next pitches were better. Her father batted them around the field.

Time for my fastball, thought Francine.

She **grip**ped the ball **firm**ly—and threw.

The ball sailed high over everything—her father, Binky, even the backstop.★

"Well," said her father, "that was certainly over the plate."

"**Way** over," said Binky.

The coach cleared his **throat**. "All right, Francine, let's give someone else a chance."

The Brain took to the mound.✳

"Ready?" asked the coach.

★ **backstop** 그물망. 경기장 밖으로 공이 나가는 것을 방지하고 관중을 보호하기 위해 홈 플레이트 뒤에 설치해 놓은 것.

✳ **mound** [야구 용어] 마운드. 투수가 공을 던질 때 서는 곳.

"In a moment," said the Brain. He licked his finger and held it up to test the wind direction. Then he began scraping the mound with his sneaker.

"Is everything all right?" asked the coach.

"Oh, yes," said the Brain. "Proper footing is very important."

When he was finally ready, the Brain made his first careful pitch.

Coach Frensky hit a grounder★ to shortstop.✳

The Brain was pleased. He checked the wind and his footing again. He did that before every pitch, so he didn't get many in.

The last ball went to right field. It was a deep pop fly.✳

"I've got it!" said Arthur, moving backward.

★ grounder [야구 용어] 땅볼. 지면 위로 굴러가는 볼을 말한다.
✳ shortstop [야구 용어] 유격수. 2루와 3루 사이의 지역을 수비하는 내야수.
✳ pop fly [야구 용어] 팝 플라이. 타자가 공을 높이 쳐올리는 것을 '플라이' 혹은 '플라이 볼'이라고 하는데, 팝 플라이는 타격한 공이 날아가는 거리가 짧으면서도 높이 뜬 공을 말한다.

He **leap**ed at what he thought was the right moment.

And **miss**ed.

The ball came down behind him.

"Almost!" said the coach. "Arthur, that was a very **graceful** leap."

Graceful? Arthur didn't feel graceful. He could feel his face getting red. He knew everyone was looking at him.

It was starting to look like the season would be a long one.

Chapter 3

Arthur stood in front of his bedroom mirror, **toss**ing a ball up and down in his **mitt**.

His father stopped in the **hall** to watch him. "Ready for your next **practice**, Arthur?" he asked.

Arthur dropped the ball. "Oh, uh . . . yeah," he said.

Mr. Read stepped into the room. "Is everything okay?"

"Um, I guess. Practices have been hard."

"Really? Tell me about them."

"I'm not very **comfortable** yet. The other

day I was playing second **base**. I **field**ed a **sharp** grounder but I couldn't get it out of my **glove**. It was like the ball was **stuck** with **glue**."

"What did you do?" his father asked.

"Well, there was a force on at second, so I took off the glove and threw it to the shortstop, who was covering the bag.★"

"Was the throw **in time**?"

Arthur **sigh**ed. "The glove was. But the ball came out along the way and **dribble**d into the **outfield**. The runner **end**ed **up** at third base."

"What did the **coach** say?" asked Mr. Read.

"He said I was **ingenious**. Very **creative**. He uses words like that a lot when I make a play."

Mr. Read sat down on the bed. "The coach

★ **bag** 베이스(base)의 구어.

has a good eye, Arthur. You just need to give it a little time."

Arthur wasn't so sure. "Everyone else just seems so far ahead of me. And I feel funny asking for help about **stuff** that everybody else knows already."

"Yes, well, most of them played last year, and you didn't. Having a **head start** makes a **difference**. I had kind of the same thing happen to me."

"You did?"

His father **nod**ded. "It was when I first got interested in cooking. Of course, I didn't know I would end up as a **cater**er. I just liked **experiment**ing with food. I was sick the first week and **miss**ed the class where the teacher **explain**ed how all the **equipment** worked. The next week I was too **shy** to ask questions. I just **pretend**ed I knew as much as everyone else."

"Did it work?" asked Arthur.

His father smiled. "For a few minutes. But then we had to make salad **dressing** in a **blend**er. Everyone else knew that the **lid** needed to be **lock**ed a certain way. I didn't. So when I turned it on . . ."

Arthur **gasp**ed.

"You guessed it. The salad dressing ended up on everything and everyone else. It was quite a **mess**."

"Did you get in trouble?"

His father **made a face**. "For a moment I thought my life was over. The teacher was covered in **goop**. He shook his **fist** at me, and goop dropped off his hand onto the **floor**."

Arthur's mouth dropped open.

"The room was perfectly **still**. And then he started to laugh. 'This,' he said, 'is a good **example** of what I was talking about—*last week.*'"

Arthur sighed. "So you **survived**."

"**Exact**ly. But I never tried to pretend I knew what I was doing again. And you shouldn't, either. Don't be **afraid** to ask for help or **advice**. You'll **catch up** soon enough."

Chapter 4

Coach Frensky was standing behind the backstop, watching his team **warm up**.

"Excuse me. Coach?"

The coach turned.

"I'm Buster's mother, Bitsy."

"Nice to meet you. Buster's a fine boy, a real **sparkplug**!"

"That's very nice to hear. I was just **wonder**ing . . . Is the ball very hard?"

"Well, no harder than any baseball."

"I see. I've just been wondering . . . What if it hits Buster?"

"Well, there's always some **risk**, but Buster's very quick. I'm sure—"

"And the baseball hats, are they made of **wool**? I think Buster's **allergic** to wool. If he's **scratch**ing, I don't think he'll be playing his best."

"We'll watch for scratching." Coach Frensky **glance**d at the **bleacher**s. "Now, I'd **recommend** you find a **seat**, um, Bitsy. You don't want all the good ones to be taken."

"Do the seats often **fill up** for **practice**?"

Coach Frensky **hesitate**d. "You never know," he said.

On the **field**, Arthur and Buster were throwing to each other. As Francine **approach**ed, Buster held up an **imaginary microphone** in front of her mouth.

"Excuse me, **Slugger**. Buster here for Action News. Think you'll top your **record** of forty-nine sky balls* today?"

"Very funny," said Francine. "At least my throws go over the plate."

"**Take it easy**," said Arthur. "You're both on the same team, remember?"

"Stay out of this, Arthur," said Francine. "You need to **concentrate** all your **attention** on holding on to the ball."

"Oh, yeah?" Arthur put his hands on his **hip**s—and the ball dropped out of his **glove**.

Francine laughed and moved onto the field.

"You know what you need, Arthur?" said Buster. "My never-**fail**, always-**succeed**s, one-hundred-percent **guarantee**d, secret good-luck **charm**."

He reached into his pocket and **produce**d a **shrivel**ed **carrot**.

★ sky ball [야구 용어] 높이 뜬 공. 하늘 높이 날아가는 타구. 보통 뜬공을 '플라이 볼(fly ball)'이라고 하는데, 특히 더 높이 올라간 경우 '스카이 볼'이라고 부른다.

Arthur **made a face**.

"Use this and you can't **miss**," said Buster. He handed the carrot to Arthur.

"You're sure about this?" asked Arthur.

"One hundred percent **absolute**ly double-sure guaranteed."

"Okay," said Arthur, and he put it in his pocket.

All during practice, Arthur **finger**ed the good-luck charm. But since no **tough** balls were hit to him, he couldn't be sure if it was working. When Francine came up to **bat**, he **crouch**ed down to be ready.

Francine **crush**ed the next **pitch** to deep right field. Arthur ran back, watching it the whole way.

"Watch the **fence**!" Buster **yell**ed.

Arthur **stop**ped **short** and looked up. The ball was coming down. He reached out to catch it.

The ball **bounce**d off his glove and went over the fence.

"Home run!" shouted Francine, rounding the **bases**.

Arthur **frown**ed.

Later, Arthur returned the carrot to Buster.

"Here," he said. "I think it's broken. Or maybe it's **run out of** luck."

Then he walked away.

Buster **examine**d the carrot and **shrug**ged. He took a **bite** and put the rest in his pocket.

Chapter

5

After **practice, Coach** Frensky **led** the team to the Sugar Bowl.

"You've been working hard," he said. "Time for a little **reward**."

Arthur was the last in, just behind Buster. It was **amazing** to him that everyone else could be so happy and **relax**ed. Most of the kids had made the same kind of **mistake**s on the **field** that he had. **Somehow** it didn't seem to **bother** them so much.

"A great practice **deserve**s ice cream!" said the coach. He went off to see about getting some tables pushed together.

"Are you **prepare**d, Arthur?" Francine asked.

Arthur eyed her **cautious**ly. "What do you mean?"

"An ice cream cone can be **tricky**. If you're not careful, you might drop it."

A lot of the kids laughed.

"Don't listen to her, Arthur," said Buster. "You're **entitle**d to ice cream just as much as the rest of us. If you want, though, I'll hold it for you."

"Thanks, Buster," said Arthur. "I think."

Once their **order**s were taken, everyone sat down. Arthur, Francine, Buster, the Brain, and Binky were all at the same table.

Francine was busy **complain**ing. "Our problem is **bat**ting," she said. "We don't have good batting."

Arthur had **struck out** twice that afternoon.

He was **swing**ing too soon, the coach had told him.

"I think we look pretty good," said Buster.

Francine laughed. "With your **eyesight**, I'm not **surprise**d."

"There's nothing wrong with my eyesight," said Buster. "I eat **plenty** of **carrot**s."

Arthur **fiddle**d with his glasses. Sometimes it was hard to **keep his eye on** the ball.

"Some people," said Binky, "have to learn how to stop the ball." He **pound**ed his **chest**. "Even if you can't keep it in your **glove**, you keep it in front of you."

Arthur looked down at his legs. Balls had passed through them so often, they felt like **goalpost**s.

"If we **concentrate** on learning the **fundamental**s," said the Brain, "our chances of winning will **improve** over time."

"I **suppose**," said Francine. "But they don't

look too good right now."

"Well," said the Brain, "it would help if you stopped throwing the ball over Fern's head."

"I didn't do that!" said Francine. "And she was standing too close, anyway."

Coach Frensky **arrived** at the table with two **pitchers** of **soda**.

"Hey!" he said, **frown**ing. "I don't want to hear any talk like that. We're a team, remember?"

Everyone **shut up**.

Coach Frensky **survey**ed the table. "Where's Arthur?" he asked.

"He was here a second ago," said Buster.

"Probably went for napkins," said Binky.

"Look!" said the Brain. He pointed out the window.

Arthur was **slink**ing up the street. A line of **drip**s from his ice cream cone **trail**ed behind him.

"I guess he wasn't in the **mood** for talk," said Francine.

"I guess not," said her father. But he stood there thinking it over for a long time.

Chapter
6

At dinner, Arthur sat quietly at the table. He **barely** touched his hamburger. He wasn't very hungry.

The same could not be said for D.W. Her hamburger was half gone, and she was **munch**ing away on corn-on-the-cob.★

"I see you **favor** the rolling **approach**," said her father.

D.W. looked **confuse**d. "What's that?"

"It's when you roll your corn around

★ **corn-on-the-cob** 옥수숫대(cob)에 붙어 있는 옥수수(corn).

before moving it down a little and rolling it some more."

D.W. stopped to look at her corn. "It's the best way," she said.

"Don't be so sure," said her mother. "Some people favor the **typewriter** approach—eating **all the way** across in a **row**, turning the **cob** a little, and then starting a new row."

D.W. **shrug**ged. "My way is better," she said.

"For you, sweetie," said her mother.

"What do you think, Arthur?" asked Mr. Read.

"Huh?"

Arthur hadn't been listening.

"Which way do you like to eat corn?" his father asked.

Arthur **sigh**ed. "Whichever way you make the fewest **mistake**s."

Mr. Read looked confused. "I'm not sure

you can make a mistake eating corn," he said. "True, you could **miss** a **kernel** here or there, but I'm not sure that really **count**s."

"Arthur's not talking about corn," said D.W. "He's talking about baseball."

"How are your **practice**s going?" asked his mother.

"Not too well," said Arthur. "I know what to do in my head. But my body doesn't always go along."

"That's perfectly **natural**," said Mr. Read. "Be **patient**, Arthur. You're paying **attention**, and that's what's important. Baseball is ninety-nine percent **concentration**."

"Sometimes it feels like everyone is concentrating on what a bad job I'm doing. Not **Coach** Frensky, though. He's always **encouraging**. He says I'm making good **progress**."

"Which parts do you feel **comfortable**

with?" asked his mother.

Arthur stopped to think. "I can throw okay. And when the ball is hit to me, I can get to the right place . . ."

"But you can't catch the ball," said D.W.

"D.W.!" said her father. "You'll catch more than a ball if you say another word."

D.W. went back to her corn.

Arthur **stare**d at his plate. "She's right," he said. "It's what everyone else says."

"**Nonsense**," said Mr. Read. "I'm sure you're making a **positive contribution**. There are probably people talking about it even now."

"You really think so?"

Mr. Read **nod**ded. "**Absolute**ly. So you'd better **eat up**. Ballplayers need their **strength**."

Arthur nodded. With their first game coming up, he wanted to be ready. He picked up his corn in both hands. With a look at D.W., he began eating it across in rows.

Chapter 7

"It's **painful**," Francine was saying. She was sitting in her living room with Muffy.

"What's painful?" Muffy asked. "No, don't tell me. It **has something to do with** baseball."

Francine was **surprise**d. "How did you know?" she asked.

"Because that's all you talk about **lately**. Double plays★ . . . making the cutoff✳ . . .

★ **double play** [야구 용어] 더블 플레이. 2명의 선수가 한꺼번에 아웃시키는 일.
✳ **cutoff** [야구 용어] 컷오프. 외야에서 홈으로 보내는 공을 내야수가 중간에 차단하는 일.

42

guarding the plate."

"Well, it's important," said Francine.

Muffy **yawn**ed. "Not to me. I could understand it better if you thought your team was **any good**."

Francine **punch**ed her **pillow**. "Don't **remind** me. Buster can't throw. The Brain takes too long for everything. And **as for** Arthur . . ." She shook her head.

"Couldn't you **promote** him or something?" said Muffy. "Make him **president** or **general** manager? Anything to get him off the **field**. My daddy's always talking about people getting **kick**ed **upstairs** in business."

Francine hadn't thought of that. "It might work. We could give Arthur lots of interesting jobs. He'd be really busy."

"Give him a **fancy** title and some **fringe** **benefit**s," said Muffy. "You know, like free **park**ing and paid **vacation**s. My daddy says those are important."

Francine was **nod**ding. "Yes, yes," she said. "Arthur would probably like all that."

"Arthur would probably like *what?*" asked her father, coming in from the kitchen.

"We were just **discuss**ing the team, Daddy."

The **coach** smiled. "We're **pull**ing **together** nicely," he said. "Still a few **kink**s, of course, but that's only **normal**."

Francine smiled at him. "Speaking of kinks, Daddy, Muffy **suggest**ed a way to get Arthur off the field: promote him to **assistant** coach."

"Oh, really?" said Mr. Frensky.

Francine **fold**ed her fingers together. "What do you say, Daddy? Please! I can't even throw straight because I'm worrying what **dumb** thing Arthur's going to do next."

"That sounds serious," said her father. "You're worried about Arthur, aren't you?"

"Why,* yes . . . Can't you see that?"

Her father stroked his chin. "It's natural for you to be concerned. After all, he is one of your best friends."

"Then you'll do it?"

Her father thought for a moment. "As coach, I have to look beyond any one player's needs. I have to consider the whole team."

"Of course," said Francine. "I think the whole team would benefit."

"You have to stand way back to get the big picture," said her father. "I may not have been seeing everything myself. Thank you, Francine."

"So you'll promote him?"

Her father shook his head. "No, no, I've got a better idea."

"Oh?" Francine didn't want a better idea.

★ why 오, 아니, 이런, 어머. 이유를 묻는 '왜'라는 의문사가 아니라, 놀라거나 의외라는 반응을 나타내는 감탄사로 쓰였다.

She liked her idea just the way it was.

Her father **rub**bed his chin. "Yes . . . **definite**ly a better idea. I'm not going to promote Arthur. I'm going to promote you instead."

"What? You mean you want to get me off the field?"

"Not **exact**ly," said her father, **grin**ning **broad**ly. "I had a different **promotion** in mind."

Francine looked at him **suspicious**ly. Whenever her father used that **tone**, something **odd was bound to** happen.

Chapter

8

Arthur stood in his **garage**, throwing a tennis ball against the wall.

Bounce-bounce-catch.

Bounce-bounce-catch.

Too bad they don't use these in the games, he thought.

"Hi, Arthur."

Francine stood in the **driveway**.

Arthur **ignore**d her.

Bounce-bounce-catch.

Bounce-bounce-catch.

"Come on, Arthur. You can't ignore me

forever."

Arthur stopped bouncing the ball.

"What brings you here, Francine? No, don't tell me. I'll **bet** you've **thought up** some new **insult**s since yesterday."

Francine's face **redden**ed. "Actually, I came over with some news. My father has made me the new **assistant coach**."

"**Congratulation**s. Would that be Assistant Coach **in Charge of Criticism**?"

"No, no . . . Look, Arthur, maybe I have gotten a little **carried away lately**. I'm sorry. But now my dad says I have to make sure the team works together."

She took out a baseball.

"And my first project is you."

"Me?" Arthur **cross**ed his arms. "What if I don't want to be a project?"

"Would you rather be **tease**d and feel **embarrass**ed all the time?"

Arthur **sigh**ed. He picked up his **glove**, and they went into the **backyard**.

"Ready?" said Francine.

She threw the ball high **overhead**.

Arthur circled **underneath** it. "I've got it! I've got it!"

The ball **land**ed five feet★ away.

Francine **smother**ed a **giggle**. "Let's try again," she said.

She picked up the ball and threw it up into the air.

Arthur **raise**d his glove.

"That's it," said Francine. "Get under it!"

Arthur **follow**ed the ball's **path**—until the sun **blind**ed him. He raised his arm to **block** the sun—and the ball hit him on the head.

"**Ouch!**"

"Well," said Francine, "at least you were

★**feet** 길이의 단위 피트. 1피트는 약 30.48센티미터이다.

under it. Look." She came over to show him. "Use your glove to keep the sun out of your eyes. That also puts the glove in a better place to catch the ball. Don't think about doing everything at once. Break it into steps."

"Oh," said Arthur. "I see."

"One more time . . ."

She threw the ball up again. This time Arthur used his glove to block the sun. He circled and circled—and caught the ball.

Arthur smiled.

Francine smiled, too.

They **practice**d a few more times.

"I think you're **get**ting **the hang of** this, Arthur."

He thought so, too.

"Thanks, Francine. You know, you might take a little **advice** yourself."

"Me? About what?"

"About **pitch**ing your fastball." He

crouched down into a catching **stance**. "Come on, **fire** it in here."

Francine threw the ball. It **sail**ed over Arthur's head, Pal's doghouse, and the **fence**.

While Francine went to get the ball, Arthur stopped to think.

"All right," said Francine, returning to her **position**. "Let's try again."

"Wait a minute," said Arthur. "You know, Francine, maybe you should think about your pitching the same way you told me to think about my catching?"

"What do you mean?"

"Breaking it into steps. Look, when you throw, you need to push off with your legs first and use your shoulder. And even after you **release** the ball, you still have to **follow through**."

"How do you know so much about it?"

Arthur looked a little embarrassed.

"Well?"

"Actually, it was D.W. I heard her **explain**ing the whole thing to my mother."

"You're telling me to take advice from D.W.?"

Arthur **shrug**ged. "Nobody has to know— **especially** D.W. What have you got to lose?"

"All right," said Francine. She got ready.

"Legs . . . shoulder . . ."

She fired the ball in at Arthur.

"Ouch!" he shouted. He pulled his hand out of his glove and shook it. "That was a real fastball."

Francine looked **please**d. "It was, wasn't it?" she said. "Thanks for the **tip**."

"You're welcome," said Arthur.

Francine **pause**d. "I really am sorry I teased you so much before."

Arthur **nod**ded. "Well, you do **overdo** it sometimes."

"If I ever overdo it again, let me know. **Deal**?"

"Deal."

"It was kind of your **fault**, though."

"My fault?" said Arthur. "How do you **figure** that?"

"Well, if you hadn't kept dropping balls, I wouldn't have teased you."

"Oh, yeah? Well at least when I throw a ball, it lands in the same **neighborhood**."

As Francine started to answer, she suddenly **froze**—and laughed.

Arthur laughed, too. "Here we go again . . . ," he said.

Chapter
9

Coach Frensky **pace**d **back and forth** in front
of his bench. "Okay, team, this is our first
game. The Penguins are pretty good, I hear."
He took a deep **breath**. "But I want you to
play just the way you have in **practice**. Just go
out and have fun."

The coach **clap**ped his hands. "Okay, team.
Let's go!"

The Eagles took the **field**. In the first
inning,★ a ball was hit **sharp**ly on the ground

★**inning** [야구 용어] 이닝. 한 회, 양 팀이 공격과 수비를 한 번씩 끝내는 동안을
말한다.

to Arthur. He fielded it cleanly and threw to second **base**.

"All right, Arthur!" said Buster.

His parents **cheer**ed from the **bleacher**s.

"That's my brother," D.W. told everyone around her. "I taught him everything he knows."

The next four innings passed quickly. Each team scored two **run**s. In the bottom★ of the fifth, Arthur came up to **bat** for the second time. He had walked before.

Now he **rap**ped a single✳ to center.

"Way to go, Arthur!" **yell**ed Francine from the bench.

Buster was next. He **foul**ed off two **pitch**es but **swung all the way** around on the third.

"Strike three!" shouted the **umpire**.

★ **bottom** [야구 용어] 한 회의 말(末).
✳ **single** [야구 용어] 단타, 1루타.

Mrs. Baxter stood up in the **stand**s and clapped. "Way to swing, Buster!" she called out.

The Brain pitched the last two innings. The sixth was **scoreless**, but in the top★ of the seventh, the Penguins scored a run to take the **lead**. Then, with one out, their fifth **batter** singled to first and reached third on an overthrow.✳

The next batter came up.

The Brain **lick**ed his finger, testing the wind **direction**.

Then he threw to the plate.

Thwack!

It was a deep fly ball.✳

"It's yours, Arthur," Francine called from

★ **top** [야구 용어] 한 회의 초(初).

✳ **overthrow** [야구 용어] 오버스로. 악송구. 공을 너무 높거나 멀리 보내 야수가 잡기에 어려운 공.

✳ **fly ball** [야구 용어] 플라이 볼. 뜬공. 높이 날아가는 타구. 평범한 플라이 볼은 수비수에 잡혀서 아웃이 되는 경우가 많다.

second base.

"I can't watch," said Buster in left field.

Arthur **backpedal**ed over the **grass**. He **blink**ed a few times, but he never took his eye off the ball. Remember what Francine said, he told himself. He **shield**ed his eyes with his glove.

Arthur reached the **fence**. The ball was coming down fast.

Plopp.

Arthur had caught it.

"**Relay**!" shouted Francine.

Arthur threw the ball. Francine caught it and **spun** around. The runner had tagged up* at third and was heading for home plate.

Binky was waiting.

"Throw it!" he called out.

★**tag up** [야구 용어] 태그 업. 타자가 친 공이 플라이 볼(fly ball)일 때, 주자가 베이스를 밟은 상태에 있다 수비팀이 그 공을 잡는 순간, 다음 베이스를 향해 달려가는 동작을 말한다.

Francine wasn't pitching, but she knew she had to throw a perfect fastball. She **plant**ed her feet **firm**ly and **fire**d to him.

The runner was **sliding** in. Binky **swept** him with the tag.★

"Out!" called the umpire.

Arthur's team **trot**ted in from the field. They were down one run, but they still had their last **turn** at bat.

The game wasn't over yet.

★ **tag** [야구 용어] 태그. 수비자가 주자에게 볼을 대서 아웃시키는 일. 야수가 날아온 공을 확실하게 잡은 상태에서 베이스나 주자를 터치하는 동작을 말한다.

Chapter 10

Everyone on the bench was watching the **field**.

Sue Ellen was up first. The first **pitch** was a ball.★

"Wait for yours!" shouted Francine.

Sue Ellen **nod**ded. She stepped back into the **batter**'s box.

In came the pitch.

Sue Ellen **swung** hard—and lined the ball into left field.

★**ball** [야구 용어] 볼. 스트라이크 존을 통과하지 않은 투구 또는 땅에 닿은 투구로, 타자가 치지 않은 공을 말한다.

Coach Frensky whistled. "All right! The tieing run's on first."

Fern was the next batter. She hit a blooper★ to right field, advancing Sue Ellen to second.

"Keep it going," said the coach.

Now Binky came to the plate. He tapped the dirt from his cleats and cocked his bat.

In came the pitch.

Binky swung hard, but a little early. The ball went deep to right field, but it was caught just before the fence. He was out, but Sue Ellen tagged up at second and ran to third.

Buster was up next.

"Just make good contact," said the coach. "A single ties it. Keep us alive."

Buster nodded.

He watched the first two pitches pass. One

★ blooper [야구 용어] 블루퍼. 힘없이 높이 뜬 플라이 볼.

ball and one strike.

The third pitch came in. Buster jumped on it.

The ball **pop**ped up a mile★ high. Everyone looked up.

The **pitcher** called for the catch.

Arthur held his **breath**. Maybe the pitcher would **trip** on the **grass** or be **blind**ed by the sun or get a sudden **itch** in his back and **scratch** it with his **glove**.

Thummp!

The ball was caught. The game was over. The Penguins had won.

Buster **trudge**d back to the **dugout** as the other team ran off the field, **cheer**ing in **victory**.

"Good **effort**, Buster," said the coach. "I thought that one was heading for the fence."

★**mile** 거리의 단위 마일. 1마일은 약 1.60934킬로미터이다.

"Me, too," said Arthur. "Good try."

Francine **storm**ed over to Buster. "Boy,★ Buster, all we needed was one little hit, and you couldn't—"

Arthur **cough**ed.

Francine looked at him. "—and you couldn't . . . have made a better try. Good job."

She **pat**ted Buster on the shoulder.

Their families **gather**ed round for a few minutes before everyone headed home.

Arthur, Francine, and Buster were the last to leave. They **replay**ed the whole game in their minds.

"We really did pretty well," said Arthur. "And the season's just starting."

"That's right," said Francine. "The next game will be better."

★ **boy** 어머나, 맙소사. 일반적으로 알고 있는 '소년'이라는 의미가 아니라, 놀라움과 안타까움을 나타내는 감탄사로 쓰였다.

Buster **shrug**ged. "I hope so," he said.

"You know, Buster," said Arthur, "Francine gave me some baseball **tip**s the other day. Maybe she could do the same for you."

"I don't know . . . ," said Buster.

"Just think about all the power you put into your Buster Ball," said Francine.

Buster **brighten**ed.

"We just need to find a way to get that power into your bat. We'll have to **get together** and—"

"What about now?" Buster asked.

"Now?" Francine looked around. The field was **empty**.

Buster **grab**bed a bat and went to home plate. "Come on, come on, what are you waiting for?"

"Arthur?" **whisper**ed Francine.

"Yes?"

"Thanks for stopping me before I **tease**d

Buster the way I teased you."

"You're welcome. And thanks for helping me with my game. See? Teamwork is the answer."

Francine nodded. "Yeah. But you know, soccer season is coming up. And if you **stink** at that, I get to tease you all over again."

With that, she went to the **pitcher**'s mound, leaving Arthur to go behind the plate.

"All right, Buster, pay **attention**. First thing we do . . ."

Arthur smiled. He wouldn't say that Francine would *never* learn.

But it **definite**ly was going to take some time.

아서,
야구팀을 만들다!

CONTENTS

아서 챕터북 소개 · 4

CHAPTER 1
● Quiz & Words List ································· 10

CHAPTER 2
● Quiz & Words List ································· 18

CHAPTER 3
● Quiz & Words List ································· 26

CHAPTER 4
● Quiz & Words List ································· 34

CHAPTER 5
● Quiz & Words List ································· 42

CHAPTER 6
● Quiz & Words List ································· 50

CHAPTER 7
● Quiz & Words List ································· 56

CHAPTER 8
● Quiz & Words List ································· 64

CHAPTER 9
● Quiz & Words List ································· 72

CHAPTER 10
● Quiz & Words List ································· 80

번역 · 88
Answer Key · 107

대한민국 영어 학습자라면 꼭 한번 읽어봐야 할, 아서 챕터북 시리즈!

아서 챕터북 시리즈(Arthur Chapter Book series)는 미국의 작가 마크 브라운(Marc Brown)이 쓴 책입니다. 레이크우드 초등학교에 다니는 주인공 아서(Arthur)가 소소한 일상에서 벌이는 다양한 에피소드를 담은 이 책은, 기본적으로 미국 초등학생들을 위해 쓰인 책이지만 누구나 공감할 만한 재미있는 스토리로 출간된 지 30년이 넘은 지금까지 남녀노소 모두에게 큰 사랑을 받고 있습니다. 아서가 주인공으로 등장하는 이야기는 리더스북과 챕터북 등 다양한 형태로 출판되었는데, 현재 미국에서만 누적 판매 부수가 6천6백만 부를 돌파한 상황으로 대한민국 인구 숫자보다 더 많은 책이 판매된 것을 생각하면 그 인기가 어느 정도 인지 실감할 수 있습니다.

특히 이『아서 챕터북』은 한국에서 영어 학습자를 위한 최적의 원서로 큰 사랑을 받고 있기도 합니다.『영어 낭독 훈련』,『잠수네 영어 학습법』,『솔빛이네 엄마표 영어연수』등 많은 영어 학습법 책들에서『아서 챕터북』을 추천 도서로 선정하고 있으며, 수많은 영어 고수들과 영어 선생님들, '엄마표 영어'를 진행하는 부모님들에게도 반드시 거쳐 가야 하는 영어원서로 전폭적인 지지를 얻고 있습니다.

번역과 단어장이 포함된 워크북, 그리고 오디오북까지 담긴 풀 패키지!

이 책은 이렇게 큰 사랑을 받고 있는 영어원서『아서 챕터북』시리즈에, 더욱 탁월한 학습 효과를 거둘 수 있도록 다양한 콘텐츠를 덧붙인 책입니다.

- 영어원서: 본문에 나온 어려운 어휘에 볼드 처리가 되어 있어 단어를 더욱 분명히 인지하며 자연스럽게 암기하게 됩니다.
- 단어장: 원서에 나온 어려운 어휘가 '한영'은 물론 '영영' 의미까지 완벽하게 정리되어 있으며, 반복되는 단어까지 넣어두어 자연스럽게 복습이 되도록 구성했습니다.
- 번역: 영어와 비교할 수 있도록 직역에 가까운 번역을 담았습니다. 원서 읽기에 익숙하지 않는 초보 학습자들도 어려움 없이 내용을 파악할 수 있습니다.
- 퀴즈: 현직 원어민 교사가 만든 이해력 점검 퀴즈가 들어있습니다.
- 오디오북: 미국 현지에서 판매중인 빠른 속도의 오디오북(분당 약 145단어)과

국내에서 녹음된 따라 읽기용 오디오북(분당 약 110단어)을 포함하고 있어 듣기 훈련은 물론 소리 내어 읽기에까지 폭넓게 사용할 수 있습니다.

이 책의 수준과 타깃 독자

- 미국 원어민 기준: 유치원 ~ 초등학교 저학년
- 한국 학습자 기준: 초등학교 저학년 ~ 중학교 1학년
- 영어원서 완독 경험이 없는 초보 영어 학습자 (토익 기준 450~750점대)
- 비슷한 수준의 다른 챕터북: Magic Tree House, Marvin Redpost, The Zack Files, Captain Underpants
- 도서 분량: 5,000단어 초반 (약 5,000~5,200단어)

아서 챕터북, 이렇게 읽어보세요!

- **단어 암기는 이렇게!** 처음 리딩을 시작하기 전, 해당 챕터에 나오는 단어들을 눈으로 쭉 훑어봅니다. 모르는 단어는 좀 더 주의 깊게 보되, 손으로 써가면서 완벽하게 암기할 필요는 없습니다. 본문을 읽으면서 이 단어들을 다시 만나게 되는데, 그 과정에서 단어의 쓰임새와 어감을 자연스럽게 익히게 됩니다. 이렇게 책을 읽은 후에, 단어를 다시 한번 복습하세요. 복습할 때는 중요하다고 생각하는 단어들을 손으로 써가면서 꼼꼼하게 외우는 것도 좋습니다. 이런 방식으로 책을 읽다보면, 많은 단어를 빠르고 부담 없이 익히게 됩니다.

- **리딩할 때는 리딩에만 집중하자!** 원서를 읽는 중간 중간 모르는 단어가 나온다고 워크북을 들춰보거나, 곧바로 번역을 찾아보는 것은 매우 좋지 않은 습관입니다. 모르는 단어나 이해가 가지 않는 문장이 나온다고 해도 펜으로 가볍게 표시만 해두고, 전체적인 맥락을 잡아가며 빠르게 읽어나가세요. 리딩을 할 때는 속도에 대한 긴장감을 잃지 않으면서 리딩에만 집중하는 것이 좋습니다. 모르는 단어와 문장은, 리딩이 끝난 후에 한꺼번에 정리해보는 '리뷰'시간을 갖습니다. 리뷰를 할 때는 번역은 물론 단어장과 사전도 꼼꼼하게 확인하면서 왜 이해가 되지 않았는지 확인해 봅니다.

- **번역 활용은 이렇게!** 이해가 가지 않는 문장은 번역을 통해서 그 의미를 파악할

수 있습니다. 하지만 한국어와 영어는 정확히 1:1 대응이 되지 않기 때문에 번역을 활용하는 데에도 지혜가 필요합니다. 의역이 된 부분까지 억지로 의미를 대응해서 암기하려고 하기보다, 어떻게 그런 의미가 만들어진 것인지 추측하면서 번역은 참고자료로 활용하는 것이 좋습니다.

- **듣기 훈련은 이렇게!** 리스닝 실력을 향상시키길 원한다면 오디오북을 적극적으로 활용하세요. 처음에는 오디오북을 틀어놓고 눈으로 해당 내용을 따라 읽으면서 훈련을 하고, 이것이 익숙해지면 오디오북만 틀어놓고 '귀를 통해' 책을 읽어보세요. 눈으로는 한 번도 읽지 않은 책을 귀를 통해 완벽하게 이해할 수 있다면 이후에는 영어 듣기로 고생하는 일은 거의 없을 것입니다.

- **소리 내어 읽고 녹음하자!** 이 책은 특히 소리 내어 읽기(Voice Reading)에 최적화된 문장 길이와 구조를 가지고 있습니다. 또한 오디오북 CD에 포함된 '따라 읽기용' 오디오북으로 소리 내어 읽기 훈련을 함께할 수 있습니다. 소리 내어 읽기를 하면서 내가 읽은 것을 녹음하고 들어보세요! 자신의 영어 발음을 들어보는 것은 몹시 민망한 일이지만, 그 과정을 통해서 의식적·무의식적으로 발음을 교정하게 됩니다. 이렇게 영어로 소리를 만들어 본 경험은 이후 탄탄한 스피킹 실력의 밑거름이 될 것입니다.

- **2~3번 반복해서 읽자!** 영어 초보자라면 2~3회 반복해서 읽을 것을 추천합니다. 초보자일수록 처음 읽을 때는 생소한 단어들과 스토리 때문에 내용 파악에 급급할 수밖에 없습니다. 하지만 일단 내용을 파악한 후에 다시 읽으면 어휘와 문장 구조 등 다른 부분까지 관찰하면서 조금 더 깊이 있게 읽을 수 있고, 그 과정에서 리딩 속도도 빨라지고 리딩 실력을 더 확고하게 다지게 됩니다.

- **'시리즈'로 꾸준히 읽자!** 한 작가의 책을 시리즈로 읽는 것 또한 영어 실력 향상에 큰 도움이 됩니다. 같은 등장인물이 다시 나오기 때문에 내용 파악이 더 수월할 뿐 아니라, 작가가 사용하는 어휘와 표현들도 자연스럽게 반복되기 때문에 탁월한 복습 효과까지 얻을 수 있습니다. 『아서 챕터북』 시리즈는 현재 10권, 총 50,000단어 분량이 출간되어 있습니다. 이 책들을 시리즈로 꾸준히 읽으면서 영어 실력을 쑥쑥 향상시켜 보세요!

영어원서 본문 구성

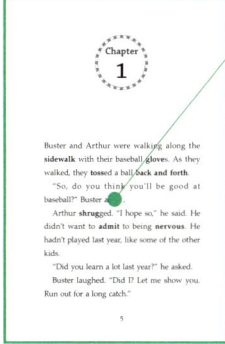

내용이 담긴 본문입니다.

원어민이 읽는 일반 원서와 같은 텍스트지만, 암기해
야 할 중요 어휘들은 볼드체로 표시되어 있습니다.
이 어휘들은 지금 들고 계신 워크북에 챕터별로 정리
되어 있습니다.

학습 심리학 연구 결과에 따르면, 한 단어씩 따로 외
우는 단어 암기는 거의 효과가 없다고 합니다. 대신
단어를 제대로 외우기 위해서는 문맥(Context) 속에
서 단어를 암기해야 하며, 한 단어 당 문맥 속에서 15
번 이상 마주칠 때 완벽하게 암기할 수 있다고 합니다.

이 책의 본문은 중요 어휘를 볼드로 강조하여, 문맥 속의 단어들을 더 확실히 인
지(Word Cognition in Context)하도록 돕고 있습니다. 또한 대부분의 중요한 단
어들은 다른 챕터에서도 반복해서 등장하기 때문에 이 책을 읽는 것만으로도 자
연스럽게 어휘력을 향상시킬 수 있습니다.

또한 본문에는 내용 이해를 돕기 위해 '각주'가 첨가
되어 있습니다. 각주는 굳이 암기할 필요는 없지만,
알아두면 내용을 더 깊이 있게 이해할 수 있어 원서
를 읽는 재미가 배가됩니다.

워크북(Workbook)의 구성

Check Your Reading Speed

해당 챕터의 단어 수가 기록되어 있어, 리딩 속도를 측정할 수 있습니다. 특히 리딩 속도를 중시하는 독자들이 유용하게 사용할 수 있습니다.

Build Your Vocabulary

본문에 볼드 표시되어 있는 단어들이 정리되어 있습니다. 리딩 전, 후에 반복해서 보면 원서를 더욱 쉽게 읽을 수 있고, 어휘력도 빠르게 향상됩니다.

단어는 〈빈도 – 스펠링 – 발음기호 – 품사 – 한글 뜻 – 영문 뜻〉 순서로 표기되어 있으며 빈도 표시(★)가 많을수록 필수 어휘입니다. 반복 등장하는 단어는 빈도 대신 '복습'으로 표기되어 있습니다. 품사는 아래와 같이 표기했습니다.

n. 명사 | **a.** 형용사 | **ad.** 부사 | **v.** 동사

conj. 접속사 | **prep.** 전치사 | **int.** 감탄사 | **idiom** 숙어 및 관용구

Comprehension Quiz

간단한 퀴즈를 통해 읽은 내용에 대한 이해력을 점검해 볼 수 있습니다.

번역

영문과 비교할 수 있도록 최대한 직역에 가까운 번역을 담았습니다.

오디오북 CD 구성

이 책은 '듣기 훈련'과 '소리 내어 읽기 훈련'을
위한 2가지 종류의 오디오북이 포함되어 있습
니다.

- 듣기 훈련용 오디오북: 분당 145단어 속도
  (미국 현지 판매 중인 오디오북)
- 소리 내어 읽기 훈련용 오디오북: 분당 110
  단어 속도

오디오북은 MP3 파일로 제공되는 MP3 기기나
컴퓨터에 옮겨서 사용하셔야 합니다. 오디오북
에 이상이 있을 경우 helper@longtailbooks.co.kr로 메일을 주시면 자세한 안내를
받으실 수 있습니다.

EBS 동영상 강의 안내

EBS의 어학사이트(EBSlang.co.kr)에서 『아서 챕터북』 동영상 강의가 진행되고 있습니다.
영어 어순의 원리에 맞게 빠르고 정확하게 이해하는 법을 완벽하게 코치해주는 국내 유일의 강의!
저렴한 수강료에 완강 시 50% 환급까지!
지금 바로 열광적인 수강 평가와 샘플 강의를 확인하세요!

http://Arthur.EnglishWish.com

Chapter 1

1. **What were Arthur and Buster doing as they walked?**

   A. They imagined playing basketball together.

   B. They were tossing a ball back and forth.

   C. They were swinging baseball bats.

   D. They were watching a baseball game.

2. **What did Buster want to show Arthur?**

   A. He wanted to show Arthur what he had learned.

   B. He wanted to show Arthur what he had lost.

   C. He wanted to show Arthur what he had bought.

   D. He wanted to show Arthur what he had seen.

3. Where did Buster's ball eventually land?

   A. A tree

   B. A gutter

   C. A roof

   D. A storm drain

4. Which of the following was NOT something that Buster said about playing baseball?

   A. Everyone would watch your every move.

   B. You would be all alone in the middle of the field.

   C. Only your teammates would watch you.

   D. There would be no place to hide.

5. How did Arthur feel about the world watching his movements?

   A. He was excited.

   B. He was nervous.

   C. He was shy.

   D. He was angry.

Check Your Reading Speed

1분에 몇 단어를 읽는지 리딩 속도를 측정해보세요.

$$\frac{557 \text{ words}}{\text{reading time ( ) sec}} \times 60 = (\quad) \text{ WPM}$$

Build Your Vocabulary

• **sidewalk** [sáidwɔ̀ːk] n. (포장한) 보도, 인도
A sidewalk is a path with a hard surface by the side of a road.

• **glove** [glʌv] n. 장갑
Gloves are pieces of clothing which cover your hands and wrists and have individual sections for each finger.

• **toss** [tɔːs] v. 던지다, 내던지다; (머리 등을) 갑자기 쳐들다
If you toss something somewhere, you throw it there lightly, often in a rather careless way.

back and forth idiom 앞뒤로, 좌우로
If someone moves back and forth, they repeatedly move in one direction and then in the opposite direction.

• **shrug** [ʃrʌg] v. (양 손바닥을 내보이면서 어깨를) 으쓱하다; n. (어깨를) 으쓱하기
If you shrug, you raise your shoulders to show that you are not interested in something or that you do not know or care about something.

⁝ **admit** [ædmít] v. 인정하다
If you admit that something bad, unpleasant, or embarrassing is true, you agree, often unwillingly, that it is true.

⁝ **nervous** [nɔ́ːrvəs] a. 겁내는, 긴장한, 두려워하는
If someone is nervous, they are frightened or worried about something that is happening or might happen, and show this in their behavior.

trot [trat] v. 빠른 걸음으로 가다; 총총걸음 치다; n. 빠른 걸음
If you trot somewhere, you move fairly fast at a speed between walking and running, taking small quick steps.

wave [weiv] v. 흔들다, 신호하다; 파도치다; n. 파도, 물결
If you wave or wave your hand, you move your hand from side to side in the air, usually in order to say hello or goodbye to someone.

farther [fά:rðər] ad. 더 멀리, 더 나아가서; a. 더 먼
Farther means more distant in especially space or time.

shoot [ʃu:t] v. (shot–shot) 힘차게 움직이다; (시선·미소 등을) 던지다; 쏘다, 발사하다; n. 사격, 발포
If someone or something shoots in a particular direction, they move in that direction quickly and suddenly.

bounce [bauns] v. 튀다, 튀게 하다; 급히 움직이다, 뛰어다니다; n. 튐, 바운드
When an object such as a ball bounces or when you bounce it, it moves upward from a surface or away from it immediately after hitting it.

branch [brænʧ] n. 나뭇가지; 지사, 분점
The branches of a tree are the parts that grow out from its trunk and have leaves, flowers, or fruit growing on them.

underneath [ʌ̀ndərní:ə] prep. ~의 밑에, 아래에; n. 밑면, 하부
If one thing is underneath another, it is directly under it, and may be covered or hidden by it.

roof [ru:f] n. 지붕; v. 지붕을 해 덮다
The roof of a building is the covering on top of it that protects the people and things inside from the weather.

follow [fάlou] v. 따라가다, 뒤따르다; ~의 뒤를 잇다
If you follow someone who is going somewhere, you move along behind them because you want to go to the same place.

gutter [gʌ́tər] n. (지붕의) 홈통, 물받이; 배수로
A gutter is a plastic or metal channel fixed to the lower edge of the roof of a building, which rain water drains into.

bottom [bátəm] n. 밑, 바닥; 기초
The bottom of something is the lowest or deepest part of it.

downspout [dáunspàut] n. 세로 홈통
A downspout is a pipe attached to the side of a building, through which water flows from the roof into a drain.

drain [drein] n. 배수관; v. 물을 빼내다, (액체가) 흘러나가다 (storm drain n. 빗물 배수관)
A drain is a pipe that carries water or sewage away from a place, or an opening in a surface that leads to the pipe.

after all idiom (예상과는 달리) 결국에는; 어쨌든
You use after all when you are saying that something that you thought might not be the case is in fact the case.

sigh [sai] v. 한숨 쉬다; n. 한숨, 탄식
When you sigh, you let out a deep breath, as a way of expressing feelings such as disappointment, tiredness, or pleasure.

amazing [əméiziŋ] a. (감탄스럽도록) 놀라운, 멋진
You say that something is amazing when it is very surprising and makes you feel pleasure, approval, or wonder.

catch on idiom 이해하다, 알다
If you catch on to something, you understand it or realize the truth of it.

field [fiːld] n. 경기장, 구장; 수비; 들, 들판; v. (공을) 잡다
A sports field is an area of grass where sports are played.

repeat [ripíːt] v. 되풀이하다, 반복하다
If you repeat something that someone else has said or written, you say or write the same thing, or tell it to another person.

crack [kræk] n. 갑작스런 날카로운 소리; 갈라진 금; v. 금이 가다, 깨다
A crack is a sharp sound, like the sound of a piece of wood breaking.

bat [bæt] ① n. 방망이, 배트; v. (야구·크리켓에서 배트로) 공을 치다 ② n. 박쥐
A bat is a specially shaped piece of wood that is used for hitting the ball in baseball, softball, cricket, rounders, or table tennis.

stare [stɛər] v. 응시하다, 뚫어지게 보다
If you stare at someone or something, you look at them for a long time.

mate [meit] n. 동료, 친구; 짝[한 쌍]의 한쪽 (teammate n. 팀원)
You can refer to someone's friends as their mates, especially when you are talking about a man and his male friends.

crowd [kraud] n. 군중, 인파; 많은 것, 다수; v. 모여들다, 붐비다
A crowd is a large group of people who have gathered together, for example to watch or listen to something interesting, or to protest about something.

stand [stænd] n. 관람석; 가판대, 좌판; v. 서다, 일어서다; 참다, 견디다
A stand at a sports ground is a large structure where people sit or stand to watch what is happening.

especially [ispéʃəli] ad. 특히, 각별히
You use especially to emphasize that what you are saying applies more to one person, thing, or area than to any others.

nod [nad] v. (고개를) 끄덕이다, 끄덕여 나타내다; n. (고개를) 끄덕임
If you nod, you move your head downward and upward to show agreement, understanding, or approval.

get something straight idiom (상황에 대한 오해가 없도록) ~을 분명히 하다
If you get something straight, you make sure that you understand it properly or that someone else does.

exciting [iksáitiŋ] a. 신나는, 흥미진진한, 흥분하게 하는
If something is exciting, it makes you feel very happy or enthusiastic.

crouch [krautʃ] v. 몸을 쭈그리다, 쪼그리고 앉다; 웅크리다; n. 웅크림
If you are crouching, your legs are bent under you so that you are close to the ground and leaning forward slightly.

stance [stæns] n. 자세, 스탠스
Your stance is the way that you are standing.

pitcher [pítʃər] ① n. 투수, 피처 ② n. 물 주전자
In baseball, the pitcher is the person who throws the ball to the batter, who tries to hit it.

matter [mǽtər] v. 중요하다; 문제되다; n. (고려하거나 처리해야 할) 문제
If you say that something does matter, you mean that it is important to you because it does have an effect on you or on a particular situation.

raise [reiz] v. 들어올리다, 들다; 키우다, 기르다
If you raise something, you move it so that it is in a higher position.

pitch [pitʃ] n. 던지기, 투구; 경기장; 최고도, 정점; v. 던지다; 처박다
In baseball, a pitch is the act of throwing a baseball by a pitcher to a batter.

blaze [bleiz] v. 타오르다; 번쩍이다, 빛나다; n. 불꽃, 화염, 섬광
When a fire blazes, it burns strongly and brightly.

swallow [swálou] v. (초조해서) 마른침을 삼키다; 삼키다, 목구멍으로 넘기다
If you swallow, you make a movement in your throat as if you are swallowing something, often because you are nervous or frightened.

tense [tens] a. 긴장한, 긴박한; 팽팽한; v. 긴장하다, 팽팽하게 하다
A tense situation or period of time is one that makes people anxious, because they do not know what is going to happen next.

exact [igzǽkt] a. 정확한, 정밀한 (exactly ad. 정확하게, 꼭)
Exact means correct in every detail.

umpire [Ámpaiər] n. (테니스·야구 경기 등의) 심판; v. 심판을 보다
An umpire is a person whose job is to make sure that a sports match or contest is played fairly and that the rules are not broken.

swing [swiŋ] v. 휘두르다, (한 점을 축으로 하여) 빙 돌다, 휙 움직이다
If something swings in a particular direction or if you swing it in that direction, it moves in that direction with a smooth, curving movement.

streak [striːk] v. (번개같이) 날쌔게 움직이다; 기다란 자국[흔적]을 내다; n. 줄무늬
If something or someone streaks somewhere, they move there very quickly.

base [beis] n. [야구] −루, 베이스; 기초, 근거, 토대
A base in baseball, softball, or rounders is one of the places at each corner of the square on the pitch.

cheer [ʧiər] n. 환호(성); v. 환호성을 지르다, 응원하다
A cheer is a shout of encouragement, approval or congratulation.

just like that idiom 쉽사리, 손쉽게
Just like that means in just the way something happened or was stated, without any or further discussion or comment.

Chapter 2

1. **Why were Buster and the others looking at the bulletin board?**
   A. They wanted to check the team rosters.
   B. They wanted to check the game times.
   C. They wanted to check where practice was held.
   D. They wanted to check the first baseball event.

2. **Who was the coach for the Eagles team?**
   A. Buster's father
   B. Muffy's father
   C. Francine's father
   D. Arthur's father

3. What was the motto of the Eagles team?

   A. Practice

   B. Teamwork

   C. Patience

   D. Confidence

4. Who was the first to pitch at their first practice?

   A. Arthur

   B. Francine

   C. Buster

   D. Muffy

5. How did the coach describe Arthur's leap?

   A. He said it was very unbalanced.

   B. He said it was very ambitious.

   C. He said it was very powerful.

   D. He said it was very graceful.

Check Your Reading Speed

1분에 몇 단어를 읽는지 리딩 속도를 측정해보세요.

$$\frac{686 \ words}{reading \ time \ (\qquad) \ sec} \times 60 = (\qquad) \ WPM$$

Build Your Vocabulary

복습 **field** [fiːld] n. 경기장, 구장; 수비; 들, 들판; v. (공을) 잡다 (ball field n. 야구장)
A sports field is an area of grass where sports are played.

* **bunch** [bʌntʃ] n. 떼, 무리; 다발, 송이; 다량
A bunch of people is a group of people who share one or more characteristics or who are doing something together.

* **huddle** [hʌdl] v. (떼 지어) 몰리다, 그러모으다; 움츠리다, 둥글게 말다; n. 군중, 무리
If people huddle together or huddle round something, they stand, sit, or lie close to each other, usually because they all feel cold or frightened.

bulletin board [búlətin bɔ́ːrd] n. 게시판
A bulletin board is a board which is usually attached to a wall in order to display notices giving information about something.

roster [rástəːr] n. 명단, 등록부
A roster is a list of the sports players who are available for a particular team.

복습 **pitch** [pitʃ] v. 던지다; 처박다; n. 던지기, 투구; 경기장; 최고도, 정점
In a game of baseball or rounders, when you pitch the ball, you throw it to the batter for them to hit it.

: **choose** [tʃuːz] v. 고르다, 선택하다
If you choose someone or something from several people or things that are available, you decide which person or thing you want to have.

. coach [kouʃ] n. 코치; v. 코치하다, 지도하다
A coach is someone who trains a person or team of people in a particular sport.

⋮ decide [disáid] v. 결정하다, 결심하다
If you decide to do something, you choose to do it, usually after you have thought carefully about the other possibilities.

work out idiom (계획 등이) 잘 되어 가다; 운동하다; (문제를) 풀다
If something works out, it happens or develops in a particular way, especially a successful way.

have on idiom ~을 입고[쓰고/신고/매고] 있다
If you have on something, you are wearing it.

. official [əfíʃəl] a. 공식의, 공인된, 공무상의
Official means approved by the government or by someone in authority.

. whisper [hwíspər] v. 속삭이다; n. 속삭임
When you whisper, you say something very quietly.

⋮ company [kʌ́mpəni] n. 친구, 함께 있음; (집에 온) 손님; 회사
Company is having another person or other people with you, usually when this is pleasant or stops you feeling lonely.

⋮ include [inklúːd] v. ~을 포함하다
If one thing includes another thing, it has the other thing as one of its parts.

⋮ grass [græs] n. 풀밭, 초원; 풀
If you talk about the grass, you are referring to an area of ground that is covered with grass, for example in your garden.

⋮ practice [prǽktis] n. 연습, 훈련; 실행, 실천; v. 연습하다; 실행하다
Practice means doing something regularly in order to be able to do it better.

¸motto [mátou] n. 좌우명, 표어, 모토
A motto is a short sentence or phrase that expresses a rule for sensible behavior, especially a way of behaving in a particular situation.

‡position [pəzíʃən] n. 위치, 자세; 입장, 처지; v. (특정한 장소에) 두다
The position of someone or something is the place where they are in relation to other things.

pitcher [pítʃər] ① n. 투수, 피처 ② n. 물 주전자
In baseball, the pitcher is the person who throws the ball to the batter, who tries to hit it.

raise [reiz] v. 들어올리다, 들다; 키우다, 기르다
If you raise something, you move it so that it is in a higher position.

‡staff [stæf] n. 부원, 직원, 스태프; v. ~에 (직원을) 배치하다
The staff of an organization are the people who work for it.

sputter [spʌ́təːr] v. 식식거리며 말하다; (엔진·불길 등이) 털털거리는 소리를 내다
If you sputter, you utter or spit out words or sounds explosively or forcibly, as when angry or confused.

‡turn [təːrn] n. 차례, 순번; 회전; 방향전환; v. 돌리다, 회전하다, 뒤엎다
If it is your turn to do something, you now have the duty, chance, or right to do it, when other people have done it before you or will do it after you.

¸reassure [riːəʃúər] v. 안심시키다
If you reassure someone, you say or do things to make them stop worrying about something.

end up idiom 마침내는 (~으로) 가다[되다]; 끝나다
If you end up doing something or end up in a particular state, you do that thing or get into that state even though you did not originally intend to.

bat [bæt] ① n. 방망이, 배트; v. (야구·크리켓에서 배트로) 공을 치다 ② n. 박쥐
A bat is a specially shaped piece of wood that is used for hitting the ball in baseball, softball, cricket, rounders, or table tennis.

prepare [pripέər] v. 준비하다, 채비하다
If you prepare something, you make it ready for something that is going to happen.

twirl [twəːrl] v. 빙빙 돌리다, 빠르게 돌다; n. 회전
If you twirl something or if it twirls, it turns around and around with a smooth, fairly fast movement.

shoot [ʃuːt] v. (shot-shot) 힘차게 움직이다; (시선·미소 등을) 던지다; 쏘다, 발사하다; n. 사격, 발포
If someone or something shoots in a particular direction, they move in that direction quickly and suddenly.

blink [bliŋk] v. 눈을 깜박거리다; (등불·별 등이) 깜박이다; n. 깜박거림
When you blink or when you blink your eyes, you shut your eyes and very quickly open them again.

nod [nad] v. (고개를) 끄덕이다, 끄덕여 나타내다; n. (고개를) 끄덕임
If you nod, you move your head downward and upward to show agreement, understanding, or approval.

ease [iːz] v. (고통·고민 등을) 진정시키다, 완화하다; n. 편함, 안정
If something unpleasant eases or if you ease it, it is reduced in degree, speed, or intensity.

wear [wɛər] v. 지치게 하다; 닳다, 낡게 하다; 입고 있다
(wear out idiom 지치게 하다, 못쓰게 되다)
If you wear someone or something out, you exhaust or tire them.

sail [seil] v. 미끄러지듯 나아가다; 항해하다; n. 배의 돛; 항해, 보트타기
If a person or thing sails somewhere, they move there smoothly and fairly quickly.

base [beis] n. [야구] –루, 베이스; 기초, 근거, 토대 (third base n. 3루)
A base in baseball, softball, or rounders is one of the places at each corner of the square on the pitch.

foul [faul] v. 파울로 치다, 파울을 범하다; a. 규칙 위반인; (성격·맛 등이) 아주 안 좋은

In a game or sport, if a player fouls another player, they touch them or block them in a way which is not allowed according to the rules.

grip [grip] v. 꽉 잡다, 움켜잡다; n. 움켜쥠, 꽉 붙잡음; 손잡이

If you grip something, you take hold of it with your hand and continue to hold it firmly.

firm [fə:rm] ① a. 굳은, 단단한; 견고한 (firmly ad. 굳게) ② n. 회사

If someone's grip is firm or if they perform a physical action in a firm way, they do it with quite a lot of force or pressure but also in a controlled way.

way [wei] ad. 큰 차이로, 훨씬; 아주 멀리; n. 방법, 방식; 길

You can use way to emphasize, for example, that something is a great distance away or is very much below or above a particular level or amount.

throat [θrout] n. 목구멍, 목 (clear one's throat idiom 목을 가다듬다, 헛기침하다)

Your throat is the back of your mouth and the top part of the tubes that go down into your stomach and your lungs.

lick [lik] v. 핥다; n. 한 번 핥기, 핥아먹기

When people or animals lick something, they move their tongue across its surface.

direction [dirékʃən] n. 방향; 지도, 지시

A direction is the general line that someone or something is moving or pointing in.

scrape [skreip] v. 문지르다; 긁다; 스쳐서 상처를 내다

If something scrapes against something else or if someone or something scrapes something else, it rubs against it, making a noise or causing slight damage.

sneaker [sníːkər] n. (pl.) 운동화

Sneakers are casual shoes with rubber soles.

proper [prápər] a. 적절한, 제대로 된; 고유의

The proper thing is the one that is correct or most suitable.

footing [fútiŋ] n. 발을 디딤; (조직 등의) 기반, 발판
You refer to your footing when you are referring to your position and how securely your feet are placed on the ground.

please [pliːz] v. 기쁘게 하다, 즐겁게 하다 (pleased a. 기뻐하는, 만족해하는)
If you are pleased, you are happy about something or satisfied with something.

leap [liːp] v. 껑충 뛰다; 뛰어넘다; n. 뜀, 도약
If you leap, you jump high in the air or jump a long distance.

miss [mis] v. (치거나 잡거나 닿지 못하고) 놓치다; (어디에 참석하지 않아서 그 일을) 놓치다
If you miss something, you fail to hit it, for example when you have thrown something at it or you have shot a bullet at it.

graceful [gréisfəl] a. 우아한, 기품 있는
Someone or something that is graceful moves in a smooth and controlled way which is attractive to watch.

Chapter 3

1. **What did Arthur do when the ball was stuck in his glove at practice?**

   A. He could not pull out the ball and gave up.

   B. He ran with the ball to shortstop.

   C. He pulled out the ball and threw it to shortstop.

   D. He took off his glove and threw it to shortstop.

2. **How did the coach feel about what Arthur did with the ball?**

   A. He said it was very foolish.

   B. He said it was very creative.

   C. He said it was very dangerous.

   D. He said it was very intelligent.

3. **Why did the other players seem to know more about baseball than Arthur?**

   A. Most of them had seen many baseball games on TV.

   B. Most of them had parents who had helped them.

   C. Most of them had played baseball last year.

   D. Most of them had dreams of being baseball players.

4. **What kind of work did Arthur's father do?**

   A. He was a teacher.

   B. He was a caterer.

   C. He was a businessman.

   D. He was a cashier.

5. **Why did Arthur's father tell him the story about his experience with a blender?**

   A. He told Arthur not to embarrass himself in front of his friends.

   B. He told Arthur not to fear making a mess when learning new things.

   C. He told Arthur to practice hard when he had time alone.

   D. He told Arthur not to pretend that he knew what he was doing.

Check Your Reading Speed

1분에 몇 단어를 읽는지 리딩 속도를 측정해보세요.

$$\frac{515 \text{ words}}{\text{reading time ( ) sec}} \times 60 = (\qquad) \text{ WPM}$$

Build Your Vocabulary

toss [tɔːs] v. 던지다, 내던지다; (머리 등을) 갑자기 쳐들다
If you toss something somewhere, you throw it there lightly, often in a rather careless way.

mitt [mit] n. 야구 글러브; 벙어리장갑
A baseball mitt is a large glove worn by a player whose job involves catching the ball.

hall [hɔːl] n. (건물의) 복도, 통로; (건물 입구 안쪽의) 현관; 넓은 방[건물]
A hall in a building is a long passage with doors into rooms on both sides of it.

practice [præktis] n. 연습, 훈련; 실행, 실천; v. 연습하다; 실행하다
Practice means doing something regularly in order to be able to do it better.

comfortable [kʌ́mfərtəbl] a. 편한, 편안한, 쾌적한
If you feel comfortable with a particular situation or person, you feel confident and relaxed with them.

base [beis] n. [야구] –루, 베이스; 기초, 근거, 토대 (second base n. 2루)
A base in baseball, softball, or rounders is one of the places at each corner of the square on the pitch.

field [fiːld] v. (공을) 잡다; n. 경기장, 구장; 수비; 들, 들판
In a game of cricket, baseball, or rounders, the team that is fielding is trying to catch the ball, while the other team is trying to hit it.

sharp [ʃɑːrp] a. (커브 등이) 급격한; (칼날 등이) 날카로운
A sharp bend or turn is one that changes direction suddenly.

glove [glʌv] n. 장갑
Gloves are pieces of clothing which cover your hands and wrists and have individual sections for each finger.

stick [stik] ① v. (stuck–stuck) 붙이다, 달라붙다; 찔러 넣다, 찌르다 ② n. 막대기
If you stick one thing to another, you attach it using glue, sticky tape, or another sticky substance.

glue [gluː] n. 풀, 접착제; v. ~을 풀[접착제]로 붙이다, 접착하다
Glue is a sticky substance used for joining things together, often for repairing broken things.

in time idiom 시간에 맞춰, 제때에; 박자를 맞추어
If you do something in time, it means that you are not late to do it.

sigh [sai] v. 한숨 쉬다; n. 한숨, 탄식
When you sigh, you let out a deep breath, as a way of expressing feelings such as disappointment, tiredness, or pleasure.

dribble [dribl] v. 공을 드리블하다; (물방울 등이) 똑똑 떨어지다
When players dribble the ball in a game such as football or basketball, they keep kicking or tapping it quickly in order to keep it moving.

outfield [áutfìːld] n. [야구] 외야, 외야수
In baseball and cricket, the outfield is the part of the field that is furthest from the batting area.

end up idiom 마침내는 (~으로) 가다[되다]; 끝나다
If you end up doing something or end up in a particular state, you do that thing or get into that state even though you did not originally intend to.

coach [koutʃ] n. 코치; v. 코치하다, 지도하다
A coach is someone who trains a person or team of people in a particular sport.

ingenious [indʒíːnjəs] a. 재간이 많은, 독창적인, 창의력이 풍부한
Something that is ingenious is very clever and involves new ideas, methods, or equipment.

creative [kriéitiv] a. 창의적인, 창조적인, 독창적인
A creative person has the ability to invent and develop original ideas, especially in the arts.

stuff [stʌf] n. 것(들); 물건, 물질; v. 채워 넣다, 속을 채우다
You can use stuff to refer to things such as a substance, a collection of things, events, or ideas, or the contents of something in a general way without mentioning the thing itself by name.

head start [héd stáːrt] n. (남보다 일찍 시작해서 갖게 되는) 유리함
If you have a head start on other people, you have an advantage over them in something such as a competition or race.

difference [dífərəns] n. 차이, 다름
The difference between two things is the way in which they are unlike each other.

nod [nad] v. (고개를) 끄덕이다, 끄덕여 나타내다; n. (고개를) 끄덕임
If you nod, you move your head downward and upward to show agreement, understanding, or approval.

cater [kéitər] v. (연회 등에) 음식·서비스를 제공하다 (caterer n. 요식업자)
If a person or company caters for an occasion such as a wedding or a party, they provide food and drink for all the people there.

experiment [ikspérəmənt] v. 실험하다; n. (과학적인) 실험
If you experiment with something or experiment on it, you do a scientific test on it in order to discover what happens to it in particular conditions.

miss [mis] v. (어디에 참석하지 않아서 그 일을) 놓치다; (치거나 잡거나 닿지 못하고) 놓치다
If you miss something such as a meeting or an activity, you do not go to it or take part in it.

explain [ikspléin] v. 설명하다, 분명하게 하다
If you explain something, you give details about it or describe it so that it can be understood.

equipment [ikwípmənt] n. 장비, 설비
Equipment consists of the things which are used for a particular purpose, for example a hobby or job.

shy [ʃai] a. 부끄러워하는, 수줍어하는
A shy person is nervous and uncomfortable in the company of other people.

pretend [priténd] v. 가장하다, ~인 체하다; a. 가짜의
If you pretend that something is the case, you act in a way that is intended to make people believe that it is the case, although in fact it is not.

dressing [drésiŋ] n. [요리] 소스, 드레싱; (상처의) 처치, 붕대
A salad dressing is a mixture of oil, vinegar, and herbs or flavorings, which you pour over salad.

blend [blend] v. 섞다, 섞이다, 혼합되다 (blender n. 믹서기, 혼합기)
If you blend substances together or if they blend, you mix them together so that they become one substance.

lid [lid] n. 뚜껑
A lid is the top of a box or other container which can be removed or raised when you want to open the container.

lock [lak] v. 잠그다; 가두어 넣다; 고정시키다; n. 자물쇠
If you lock something or someone in a place, room, or container, you put them there and fasten the lock.

gasp [gæsp] v. 숨이 턱 막히다, 헉 하고 숨을 쉬다; n. (숨이 막히는 듯) 헉 하는 소리를 냄
When you gasp, you take a short quick breath through your mouth, especially when you are surprised, shocked, or in pain.

mess [mes] n. 엉망진창, 난잡함; v. 망쳐놓다, 방해하다
If you say that something is a mess or in a mess, you think that it is in an untidy state.

make a face idiom 얼굴을 찌푸리다, 침울한 표정을 짓다
If you make a face, you twist your face to indicate a certain mental or emotional state.

goop [gu:p] n. 끈적끈적 들러붙는 것
Goop is a thick, slimy substance.

fist [fist] n. (쥔) 주먹
Your hand is referred to as your fist when you have bent your fingers in toward the palm in order to hit someone.

floor [flɔ:r] n. 바닥, 마루; 층
The floor of a room is the part of it that you walk on.

still [stil] a. 정지한, 움직이지 않는; 조용한, 고요한; ad. 여전히, 아직도
If you stay still, you stay in the same position and do not move.

example [igzǽmpl] n. (대표적인) 본보기, 전형; (설명·증명을 위한) 예, 사례
An example of a particular class of objects or styles is something that has many of the typical features of such a class or style, and that you consider clearly represents it.

survive [sərváiv] v. 살아남다, 생존하다
If a person or living thing survives in a dangerous situation such as an accident or an illness, they do not die.

exact [igzǽkt] a. 정확한, 정밀한 (exactly ad. 정확하게, 꼭)
Exact means correct in every detail.

afraid [əfréid] a. 두려워하여, 걱정하는; ~할 용기가 없는
If you are afraid of someone or afraid to do something, you are frightened because you think that something very unpleasant is going to happen to you.

advice [ædváis] n. 충고, 조언
If you give someone advice, you tell them what you think they should do in a particular situation.

catch up idiom 따라잡다, 따라가다

If you catch up with someone or something, you reach the same level or standard as them that was better or more advanced.

Chapter 4

1. **How did Buster's mother feel about Buster playing baseball?**

   A. She thought that he was tough and could handle it.

   B. She thought that Buster was very popular with the team.

   C. She thought that Buster was improving very quickly.

   D. She worried about Buster's safety while playing baseball.

2. **What did Francine say that Arthur needed to concentrate on?**

   A. She told him that he needed to concentrate on avoiding the ball.

   B. She told him that he needed to concentrate on throwing the ball.

   C. She told him that he needed to concentrate on holding the ball.

   D. She told him that he needed to concentrate on catching the ball.

3. **Why did Buster give Arthur a shriveled carrot?**

   A. Arthur looked hungry.

   B. It was Buster's good-luck charm.

   C. Carrots were good for your eyesight.

   D. Buster wanted to throw it away.

4. **What happened when Francine hit the ball to Arthur?**

   A. He caught it and threw it to the pitcher.

   B. He caught it but dropped it out of his glove.

   C. He tried to catch it but it bounced out of his glove.

   D. He tried to catch it but he ran into the fence.

5. **How did Arthur feel about what Buster had given him?**

   A. He felt that it was broken.

   B. He felt that it was delicious.

   C. He felt that it brought him luck.

   D. He felt that it improved his abilities.

1분에 몇 단어를 읽는지 리딩 속도를 측정해보세요.

$$\frac{467 \text{ words}}{\text{reading time ( ) sec}} \times 60 = (\quad) \text{ WPM}$$

Build Your Vocabulary

coach [kouʧ] n. 코치; v. 코치하다, 지도하다
A coach is someone who trains a person or team of people in a particular sport.

warm up idiom (스포츠나 활동 전에) 몸을 천천히 풀다, 준비 운동을 하다
If you warm up for an event such as a race, you prepare yourself for it by doing exercises or by practicing just before it starts.

sparkplug [spá:rkplʌg] n. 중심적 인물; v. 주역을 맡아 하다
A sparkplug is a person who leads, inspires, or animates someone or something.

wonder [wʌ́ndər] v. 호기심을 가지다, 이상하게 여기다; n. 경탄할 만한 것, 경이
If you wonder about something, you think about it because it interests you and you want to know more about it.

risk [risk] n. 위험; v. (~을) 위태롭게 하다, ~의 위험을 무릅쓰다
If there is a risk of something unpleasant, there is a possibility that it will happen.

wool [wul] n. 모직물; 양모, 양털
Wool is a material made from animal's wool that is used to make things such as clothes, blankets, and carpets.

allergic [əlɔ́:rdʒik] a. 알레르기 체질인, ~에 민감한
If you are allergic to something, you become ill or get a rash when you eat it, smell it, or touch it.

scratch [skrætʃ] v. 긁다, 할퀴다; n. 생채기, 할큄, 찰과상
If you scratch yourself, you rub your fingernails against your skin because it is itching.

glance [glæns] v. 흘낏 보다, 잠깐 보다; n. 흘낏 봄
If you glance at something or someone, you look at them very quickly and then look away again immediately.

bleacher [blíːtʃər] n. (pl.) (지붕 없는) 야외 관람석
The bleachers are a part of an outdoor sports stadium, or the seats in that area, which are usually uncovered and are the least expensive place where people can sit.

recommend [rèkəménd] v. 권하다, 추천하다
If someone recommends a person or thing to you, they suggest that you would find that person or thing good or useful.

seat [siːt] n. (앉을 수 있는) 자리, 좌석; v. 앉히다
A seat is an object that you can sit on, for example a chair.

fill up idiom (~으로) 가득 차다, ~을 가득 채우다
If a container or a place fills, it becomes completely full.

practice [prǽktis] n. 연습, 훈련; 실행, 실천; v. 연습하다; 실행하다
Practice means doing something regularly in order to be able to do it better.

hesitate [hézətèit] v. 주저하다, 머뭇거리다, 망설이다
If you hesitate, you do not speak or act for a short time, usually because you are uncertain, embarrassed, or worried about what you are going to say or do.

field [fiːld] n. 경기장, 구장; 수비; 들, 들판; v. (공을) 잡다
A sports field is an area of grass where sports are played.

approach [əpróutʃ] v. 접근하다, 다가오다; n. 접근, 가까움
When you approach something, you get closer to it.

⁑ imaginary [imǽdʒənèri] a. 상상의, 가공의
An imaginary person, place, or thing exists only in your mind or in a story, and not in real life.

. microphone [máikrəfòun] n. 마이크(로폰)
A microphone is a device that is used to make sounds louder or to record them on a tape recorder.

slugger [slʌ́gər] n. (야구·권투의) 강타자
In baseball, a slugger is a player who hits the ball very hard.

⁑ record [rékərd] n. (운동 경기 등의) 기록, 경력, 이력; v. 기록하다
A record is the best result that has ever been achieved in a particular sport or activity, for example the fastest time, the furthest distance, or the greatest number of victories.

take it easy idiom 진정해라
If someone tells you to take it easy, they mean that you should relax and not do very much at all.

⁑ concentrate [kánsəntrèit] v. 집중하다, 전념하다
If you concentrate on something, you give all your attention to it.

⁑ attention [əténʃən] n. 주의, 관심; 배려
If you give someone or something your attention, you look at it, listen to it, or think about it carefully.

. hip [hip] n. 허리, 둔부, 엉덩이
Your hips are the two areas at the sides of your body between the tops of your legs and your waist.

글 glove [glʌv] n. 장갑
Gloves are pieces of clothing which cover your hands and wrists and have individual sections for each finger.

⁑ fail [feil] v. 실패하다, ~하지 못하다; 도움을 못 주다, 실망시키다
If you fail to do something that you were trying to do, you are unable to do it or do not succeed in doing it.

succeed [səksíːd] v. 성공하다; 뒤를 잇다
If you succeed in doing something, you manage to do it.

guarantee [gærəntíː] v. 보증하다, 다짐하다; n. 보증, 개런티
If you guarantee something, you promise that it will definitely happen, or that you will do or provide it for someone.

charm [ʧɑːrm] n. 마법, 부적; 매력; v. 주문[마법]을 걸다; 매혹하다
A charm is an act, saying, or object that is believed to have magic powers.

produce [prədjúːs] v. (~에서) 꺼내 보이다, 보여 주다; 생산하다; n. 생산물
If you produce an object from somewhere, you show it or bring it out so that it can be seen.

shrivel [ʃrívəl] v. 쪼글쪼글해지다, 시들게 하다
When something shrivels or when something shrivels it, it becomes dryer and smaller, often with lines in its surface, as a result of losing the water it contains.

carrot [kǽrət] n. 당근; 보상, 미끼
Carrots are long, thin, orange-colored vegetables.

make a face idiom 얼굴을 찌푸리다, 침울한 표정을 짓다
If you make a face, you twist your face to indicate a certain mental or emotional state.

miss [mis] v. (치거나 잡거나 닿지 못하고) 놓치다; (어디에 참석하지 않아서 그 일을) 놓치다
If you miss something, you fail to hit it, for example when you have thrown something at it or you have shot a bullet at it.

absolute [ǽbsəluːt] a. 완전한, 무조건의, 절대적인 (absolutely ad. 절대적으로, 무조건)
Absolute means total and complete.

finger [fíŋgər] v. 손으로 만지다, 더듬다; n. 손가락
If you finger something, you touch or feel it with your fingers.

tough [tʌf] a. 곤란한, 어려운; 강인한; 억센; 엄한, 냉정한
A tough task or problem is difficult to do or solve.

복습 bat [bæt] ① v. (야구·크리켓에서 배트로) 공을 치다; n. 방망이, 배트; ② n. 박쥐
When you bat, you have a turn at hitting the ball with a bat in baseball, softball, cricket, or rounders.

복습 crouch [krautʃ] v. 몸을 쭈그리다, 쪼그리고 앉다; 웅크리다; n. 웅크림
If you are crouching, your legs are bent under you so that you are close to the ground and leaning forward slightly.

crush [krʌʃ] v. 밀어 넣다; 잔뜩 구겨지다; 으스러뜨리다
If you are crushed against someone or something, you are pushed or pressed against them.

복습 pitch [pitʃ] n. 던지기, 투구; 경기장; 최고도, 정점; v. 던지다; 처박다
In baseball, a pitch is the act of throwing a baseball by a pitcher to a batter.

fence [fens] n. 울타리, 담; v. 둘러막다
A fence is a barrier between two areas of land, made of wood or wire supported by posts.

yell [jel] v. 소리치다, 고함치다; n. 고함소리, 부르짖음
If you yell, you shout loudly, usually because you are excited, angry, or in pain.

stop short idiom (하던 일을) 갑자기 멈추다, 중단시키다
If you stop short or stop someone short, you suddenly stop doing it or make them stop doing it.

복습 bounce [bauns] v. 튀다, 튀게 하다; 급히 움직이다, 뛰어다니다; n. 튐, 바운드
When an object such as a ball bounces or when you bounce it, it moves upward from a surface or away from it immediately after hitting it.

복습 base [beis] n. [야구] −루, 베이스; 기초, 근거, 토대
A base in baseball, softball, or rounders is one of the places at each corner of the square on the pitch.

frown [fraun] v. 얼굴[눈살]을 찌푸리다; n. 찡그림, 찌푸림
When someone frowns, their eyebrows become drawn together, because they are annoyed or puzzled.

run out of ~ idiom ~을 다 써버리다, 동나다, 다하다
If a person or a machine runs out of a supply of something, they finish it or use it all up.

examine [igzǽmin] v. 살펴보다, 검사하다; 시험하다
If you examine something, you look at it carefully.

shrug [ʃrʌg] v. (양 손바닥을 내보이면서 어깨를) 으쓱하다; n. (어깨를) 으쓱하기
If you shrug, you raise your shoulders to show that you are not interested in something or that you do not know or care about something.

bite [bait] n. 한 입(의 분량); 물기, 물어뜯기; v. 물다, 물어뜯다
A bite is the amount of food you take into your mouth when you bite it.

Chapter 5

1. **Why was it amazing to Arthur that everyone else on the team seemed so relaxed?**

   A. They had played perfectly without any mistakes.

   B. They had made the same mistakes but did not seem bothered.

   C. They had spent a lot of energy playing very hard during practice.

   D. They should have been upset about losing their first game.

2. **Why did the coach bring the team to the Sugar Bowl?**

   A. He had a coupon for free ice cream there.

   B. He thought that ice cream helped recover their energy.

   C. He thought that a great practice deserved ice cream.

   D. He brought them there to meet their parents.

3. **What did Francine say about Arthur and ice cream?**

    A. She said that he had to be careful or he might drop it.

    B. She said that he had to be quick or it might melt.

    C. She said that he did not deserve to eat ice cream.

    D. She said that ice cream would not help him improve.

4. **What did Buster say about his eyesight?**

    A. He said there was nothing wrong because he wore contact lenses.

    B. He said there was nothing wrong because he wore glasses.

    C. He said there was nothing wrong because he took vitamins.

    D. He said there was nothing wrong because he ate plenty of carrots.

5. **How did the coach feel when Arthur left?**

    A. He thought that Arthur went to get napkins.

    B. He thought that Arthur went to practice more.

    C. He thought that Arthur was not in the mood to talk.

    D. He thought that Arthur was not in the mood for ice cream.

Check Your Reading Speed

1분에 몇 단어를 읽는지 리딩 속도를 측정해보세요.

$$\frac{480 \text{ words}}{\text{reading time ( ) sec}} \times 60 = (\text{) WPM}$$

Build Your Vocabulary

practice [prǽktis] n. 연습, 훈련; 실행, 실천; v. 연습하다; 실행하다
Practice means doing something regularly in order to be able to do it better.

coach [koutʃ] n. 코치; v. 코치하다, 지도하다
A coach is someone who trains a person or team of people in a particular sport.

lead [li:d] ① v. (led–led) 이끌다, 인솔하다; n. 선도, 지휘 ② n. [광물] 납
If you lead someone to a particular place or thing, you take them there.

reward [riwɔ́:rd] n. 보상, 보답; 현상금; v. 보답하다, 보상하다
A reward is something that you are given, for example because you have behaved well, worked hard, or provided a service to the community.

amazing [əméiziŋ] a. (감탄스럽도록) 놀라운, 멋진
You say that something is amazing when it is very surprising and makes you feel pleasure, approval, or wonder.

relax [rilǽks] v. (긴장·힘 등을) 풀다, 편하게 되다 (relaxed a. 편안한, 긴장이 풀린)
If you relax or if something relaxes you, you feel more calm and less worried.

mistake [mistéik] n. 실수, 잘못; v. 잘못 판단하다, 틀리다
If you make a mistake, you do something which you did not intend to do, or which produces a result that you do not want.

field [fiːld] n. 경기장, 구장; 수비; 들, 들판; v. (공을) 잡다
A sports field is an area of grass where sports are played.

somehow [sʌ́mhàu] ad. 왠지, 아무래도; 여하튼, 어쨌든
You use somehow to say that you do not know or cannot say how something was done or will be done.

bother [bɑ́ðər] v. 신경 쓰이게 하다, 괴롭히다; 신경 쓰다, 애를 쓰다; n. 성가심
If something bothers you, or if you bother about it, it worries, annoys, or upsets you.

deserve [dizə́ːrv] v. ~을 할[받을] 만하다, ~할 가치가 있다
If you say that a person or thing deserves something, you mean that they should have it or receive it because of their actions or qualities.

prepare [pripɛ́ər] v. 준비하다, 채비하다
If you prepare something, you make it ready for something that is going to happen.

cautious [kɔ́ːʃəs] a. 조심스러운, 신중한 (cautiously ad. 조심스럽게)
Someone who is cautious acts very carefully in order to avoid possible danger.

tricky [tríki] a. 교묘한, 까다로운
If you describe a task or problem as tricky, you mean that it is difficult to do or deal with.

entitle [intáitl] v. 권리[자격]를 주다; 제목을 붙이다, 칭하다
If you entitle someone to something, you give them a right to have or do it.

order [ɔ́ːrdər] n. 주문; 명령; 순서; v. 주문하다; 명령을 내리다
An order is a request for something to be brought, made, or obtained for you in return for money.

complain [kəmpléin] v. 불평하다, 투덜거리다
If you complain about a situation, you say that you are not satisfied with it.

bat [bæt] ① v. (야구·크리켓에서 배트로) 공을 치다; n. 방망이, 배트 ② n. 박쥐
When you bat, you have a turn at hitting the ball with a bat in baseball, softball, cricket, or rounders.

strike out idiom [야구] 삼진당하다, 삼진시키다
If you strike out, you fail to hit the ball successfully three times and so finish your turn or make someone do this.

swing [swiŋ] v. 휘두르다, (한 점을 축으로 하여) 빙 돌다, 휙 움직이다
If something swings in a particular direction or if you swing it in that direction, it moves in that direction with a smooth, curving movement.

eyesight [áisàit] n. 시력, 시야
Your eyesight is your ability to see.

surprise [sərpráiz] v. 놀라게 하다, 경악하게 하다 (surprised a. 매우 놀란)
If you surprise someone, you give them, tell them, or do something they are not expecting.

plenty [plénti] n. 많음, 가득, 풍부한 양
If there is plenty of something, there is a large amount of it.

carrot [kǽrət] n. 당근; 보상, 미끼
Carrots are long, thin, orange-colored vegetables.

fiddle [fidl] v. 만지작거리다; 바이올린을 켜다; n. 바이올린
If you fiddle with an object, you keep moving it or touching it with your fingers.

keep an eye on idiom ~을 계속 지켜보다
If you keep an eye on someone or something, you watch them or it carefully.

pound [paund] v. 마구 치다, 세게 두드리다; 쿵쿵 울리다; n. 타격
If you pound something or pound on it, you hit it with great force, usually loudly and repeatedly.

chest [tʃest] ① n. 가슴, 흉부 ② n. 상자, 궤
Your chest is the top part of the front of your body where your ribs, lungs, and heart are.

glove [glʌv] n. 장갑
Gloves are pieces of clothing which cover your hands and wrists and have individual sections for each finger.

goalpost [góulpòust] n. 골대
A goalpost is one of the two upright wooden posts that are connected by a crossbar and form the goal in games such as football and rugby.

concentrate [kánsəntrèit] v. 집중하다, 전념하다
If you concentrate on something, you give all your attention to it.

fundamental [fʌndəméntəl] n. (pl.) 근본, 기초; 원리, 원칙; a. 기초의, 근본적인
You use fundamental to describe things, activities, and principles that are very important or essential.

improve [imprúːv] v. 개선하다, 진보하다, 나아지다
If something improves or if you improve it, it gets better.

suppose [səpóuz] v. (~이라고) 생각하다, 믿다; 가정하다
If you suppose that something is true, you believe that it is probably true, because of other things that you know.

arrive [əráiv] v. 도착하다, 이르다, 도달하다
When a person or vehicle arrives at a place, they come to it at the end of a journey.

pitcher [pítʃər] ① n. 물 주전자 ② n. 투수, 피처
A pitcher is a jug.

soda [sóudə] n. 탄산음료
Soda is a sweet fizzy drink.

frown [fraun] v. 얼굴[눈살]을 찌푸리다; n. 찡그림, 찌푸림
When someone frowns, their eyebrows become drawn together, because they are annoyed or puzzled.

shut up idiom 입을 다물다
If someone shuts up, they cease to talk or make a noise or cause to cease to talk or make a noise.

* **survey** [sərvéi] v. 둘러보다, 바라보다; 조사하다; n. 조사
If you survey something, you look at or consider the whole of it carefully.

slink [sliŋk] v. 살금살금 걷다, 몰래 도망가다
If you slink somewhere, you move there quietly because you do not want to be seen.

* **drip** [drip] n. 방울져 떨어지는 것, (물)방울; v. 방울방울[뚝뚝] 떨어지다; 흐르다
A drip is a small individual drop of a liquid.

* **trail** [treil] v. ~을 뒤쫓다; (보통 땅에 대고 뒤로) 끌다, 끌리다; n. 지나간 자국, 흔적
If you trail something or it trails, it hangs down loosely behind you as you move along.

* **mood** [muːd] n. 기분, 심정; 분위기
Your mood is the way you are feeling at a particular time. If you are in a good mood, you feel cheerful.

Chapter 6

1. **What was the rolling approach when eating corn?**

   A. It was when you rolled the corn around before moving it down.

   B. It was when you rolled the corn into other food on your plate.

   C. It was when you ate the corn straight across in rows.

   D. It was when you rolled butter onto a corn cob.

2. **How did Arthur answer when asked how he liked eating corn?**

   A. He said that he liked the typewriter approach.

   B. He said that he liked the rolling approach.

   C. He said that he liked whichever way other people liked.

   D. He said that he liked whichever way made the fewest mistakes.

3. **Which of the following was NOT a way that Arthur felt about baseball practices?**

   A. He felt that he knew what to do in his head.

   B. He felt that practices were going very well.

   C. He felt that the coach was always encouraging.

   D. He felt that everyone was concentrating on what a bad job he did.

4. **What did D.W. say Arthur could not do?**

   A. She said that Arthur could not throw.

   B. She said that Arthur could not run.

   C. She said that Arthur could not catch.

   D. She said that Arthur could not hit.

5. **Why did Arthur eat his corn in the end?**

   A. He wanted to show his father his appreciation for the meal.

   B. He wanted to be ready with strength for his first game.

   C. He wanted to be excused from the dinner table.

   D. He wanted to beat D.W. in an eating contest.

Check Your Reading Speed

1분에 몇 단어를 읽는지 리딩 속도를 측정해보세요.

$$\frac{436 \text{ words}}{\text{reading time (} \quad \text{) sec}} \times 60 = (\quad) \text{ WPM}$$

Build Your Vocabulary

barely [béərli] ad. 간신히, 가까스로, 빠듯하게
You use barely to say that something is only just true or only just the case.

munch [mʌntʃ] v. 우적우적 먹다
If you munch food, you eat it by chewing it slowly, thoroughly, and rather noisily.

favor [féivər] v. 더 좋아하다, 선호하다; 편들다; n. 호의; 친절한 행위
If you favor something, you prefer it to the other choices available.

approach [əpróutʃ] n. 접근, 가까움; v. 접근하다, 다가오다
Approach is the act of drawing spatially closer to something.

confuse [kənfjúːz] v. 어리둥절하게 하다, 혼동하다 (confused a. 당황한, 어리둥절한)
To confuse someone means to make it difficult for them to know exactly what is happening or what to do.

typewriter [táipràitər] n. 타자기
A typewriter is a machine with keys which are pressed in order to print letters, numbers, or other characters onto paper.

all the way idiom 완전히; 내내, 줄곧
All the way means completely.

row [rou] ① n. 열, 줄; 좌석 줄 ② v. 노[배]를 젓다
A row of things or people is a number of them arranged in a line.

cob [kab] n. 옥수숫대
Cobs are the long rounded parts of the maize or corn plant on which small yellow seeds grow, and which is eaten as a vegetable.

shrug [ʃrʌg] v. (양 손바닥을 내보이면서 어깨를) 으쓱하다; n. (어깨를) 으쓱하기
If you shrug, you raise your shoulders to show that you are not interested in something or that you do not know or care about something.

sigh [sai] v. 한숨 쉬다; n. 한숨, 탄식
When you sigh, you let out a deep breath, as a way of expressing feelings such as disappointment, tiredness, or pleasure.

mistake [mistéik] n. 실수, 잘못; v. 잘못 판단하다, 틀리다
If you make a mistake, you do something which you did not intend to do, or which produces a result that you do not want.

miss [mis] v. (치거나 잡거나 닿지 못하고) 놓치다; (어디에 참석하지 않아서 그 일을) 놓치다
If you miss something, you fail to hit it, for example when you have thrown something at it or you have shot a bullet at it.

kernel [kə:rnl] n. (견과류의) 알맹이, 중심부; 핵심, 요점
The kernel of a nut is the part that is inside the shell.

count [kaunt] v. 중요하다; 계산하다, 셈하다; n. 계산
If something or someone counts for something or counts, they are important or valuable.

practice [præktis] n. 연습, 훈련; 실행, 실천; v. 연습하다; 실행하다
Practice means doing something regularly in order to be able to do it better.

natural [nætʃərəl] a. 당연한, 자연스러운; 자연의, 천연의
If you say that it is natural for someone to act in a particular way or for something to happen in that way, you mean that it is reasonable in the circumstances.

patient [péiʃənt] a. 인내심[참을성] 있는; n. 환자
If you are patient, you stay calm and do not get annoyed, for example when something takes a long time, or when someone is not doing what you want them to do.

attention [əténʃən] n. 주의, 관심; 배려
If you give someone or something your attention, you look at it, listen to it, or think about it carefully.

concentrate [kánsəntrèit] v. 집중하다, 전념하다 (concentration n. 집중)
If you concentrate on something, you give all your attention to it.

coach [koutʃ] n. 코치; v. 코치하다, 지도하다
A coach is someone who trains a person or team of people in a particular sport.

encourage [inkə́:ridʒ] v. 격려하다, 용기를 북돋우다 (encouraging a. 격려하는)
If you encourage someone, you give them confidence, hope, or support.

progress [prágres] n. 진보, 향상; 전진, 진행; v. 진보하다; 진행하다
Progress is the process of gradually improving or getting nearer to achieving or completing something.

comfortable [kʌ́mfərtəbl] a. 편한, 편안한, 쾌적한
If you feel comfortable with a particular situation or person, you feel confident and relaxed with them.

stare [stɛər] v. 응시하다, 뚫어지게 보다
If you stare at someone or something, you look at them for a long time.

nonsense [nánsens] n. 허튼소리; 바보 같은 짓; a. 어리석은, 무의미한
If you say that something spoken or written is nonsense, you mean that you consider it to be untrue or silly.

positive [pázitiv] a. 긍정적인; 명확한, 확신하고 있는
A positive fact, situation, or experience is pleasant and helpful to you in some way.

contribution [kàntrəbjúːʃən] n. 공헌, 기여; 기부, 기증
If you make a contribution to something, you do something to help make it successful or to produce it.

nod [nad] v. (고개를) 끄덕이다, 끄덕여 나타내다; n. (고개를) 끄덕임
If you nod, you move your head downward and upward to show agreement, understanding, or approval.

absolute [ǽbsəluːt] a. 완전한, 무조건의, 절대적인 (absolutely ad. 절대적으로, 무조건)
Absolute means total and complete.

eat up idiom (~을) 다 먹다
If you eat up, you eat all the food you have been given.

strength [streŋkθ] n. 힘, 기운
Your strength is the physical energy that you have, which gives you the ability to perform various actions, such as lifting or moving things.

Chapter

7

1. **How did Muffy know that the painful thing that Francine mentioned involved baseball?**
   A. Baseball was all that Muffy wanted to talk about lately.
   B. Baseball was all that Francine talked about lately.
   C. Muffy was interested in joining the team and had asked Francine earlier.
   D. Francine had been injured during baseball practice earlier.

2. **What did Muffy suggest that Francine should do for Arthur?**
   A. Muffy suggested that Francine should cut Arthur from the team.
   B. Muffy suggested that Francine should promote Arthur to get him off the field.
   C. Muffy suggested that Francine should talk to Arthur's dad.
   D. Muffy suggested that Francine should coach Arthur.

3. How did Francine think that Arthur would feel about Muffy's suggestion?

    A. She thought that Arthur was probably already thinking the same way.

    B. She thought that Arthur would probably suggest the same for Muffy instead.

    C. She thought that Arthur would probably ignore the suggestion.

    D. She thought that Arthur would probably like the suggestion.

4. Who did the coach have to consider before making his decision?

    A. Arthur's feelings

    B. Arthur's workload

    C. The whole team's needs

    D. Francine's happiness

5. What did the coach decide to do?

    A. He decided to promote Arthur like Francine had suggested.

    B. He decided to coach Arthur more one-on-one.

    C. He decided to cut Arthur from the team.

    D. He decided to promote Francine instead.

Check Your Reading Speed

1분에 몇 단어를 읽는지 리딩 속도를 측정해보세요.

$$\frac{495 \ words}{reading \ time \ (\quad) \ sec} \times 60 = (\quad) \ WPM$$

Build Your Vocabulary

painful [péinfəl] a. 아픈; 괴로운, 골치 아픈
If something such as an illness, injury, or operation is painful, it causes you a lot of physical pain.

have something to do with idiom ~와 관계가 있다
If one thing has something to do with another thing, it is connected or concerned with it.

surprise [sərpráiz] v. 놀라게 하다, 경악하게 하다 (surprised a. 매우 놀란)
If you surprise someone, you give them, tell them, or do something they are not expecting.

lately [léitli] ad. 요즘에, 최근에, 근래
You use lately to describe events in the recent past, or situations that started a short time ago.

guard [ga:rd] v. 지키다, 보호하다, 경비를 보다; n. 경비 요원, 보초
If you guard a place, person, or object, you stand near them in order to watch and protect them.

yawn [jɔːn] v. 하품하다; n. 하품
If you yawn, you open your mouth very wide and breathe in more air than usual, often when you are tired or when you are not interested in something.

any good idiom 조금은 도움이 되는, 쓸 만한
If someone or something is not any good, they are not satisfactory or are of a low standard.

.**punch** [pʌntʃ] v. 강타하다, 두드리다; (키를) 입력하다; n. 주먹질, 펀치
If you punch someone or something, you hit them hard with your fist.

.**pillow** [pílou] n. 베개; 머리 받침대
A pillow is a rectangular cushion which you rest your head on when you are in bed.

:**remind** [rimáind] v. 생각나게 하다, 상기시키다, 일깨우다
If someone reminds you of a fact or event that you already know about, they say something which makes you think about it.

as for idiom ~에 대해서 말하자면
You use as for at the beginning of a sentence in order to introduce a slightly different subject that is still connected to the previous one.

.**promote** [prəmóut] v. 승진시키다; 진전시키다, 촉진하다
If someone is promoted, they are given a more important job or rank in the organization that they work for.

:**president** [prézədənt] n. 장(長), 회장; 대통령
The president of an organization is the person who has the highest position in it.

:**general** [dʒénərəl] a. (신분·권한 등의) 최상위의; 대체적인, 일반적인
(general manager n. [야구] 단장)
General is used to describe a person's job, usually as part of their title, to indicate that they have complete responsibility for the administration of an organization or business.

field [fiːld] n. 경기장, 구장; 수비; 들, 들판; v. (공을) 잡다
A sports field is an area of grass where sports are played.

kick someone upstairs idiom ~를 이름뿐인 높은 자리에 앉히다
If you kick someone upstairs, you move them to a job that seems to be more important but which actually has less power or influence.

fancy [fǽnsi] a. 화려한, 고급스러운; v. 원하다, ~하고 싶다; n. 공상, 상상
If you describe something as fancy, you mean that it is very expensive or of very high quality.

fringe [frindʒ] a. (중요성 등이) 부차적인; n. (숄·테이블 가장자리의) 술, 술 장식; v. ~에 술을 달다
Fringe groups or events are less important or popular than other related groups or events.

benefit [bénəfit] n. 혜택, 이득; v. 이익을 얻다, 득을 보다 (fringe benefit n. 부가 수당)
Fringe benefits are extra things that some people get from their job in addition to their salary, for example a car.

park [pɑːrk] v. 주차하다; n. 주차장; 공원 (free parking n. 무료 주차)
When you park a vehicle or park somewhere, you drive the vehicle into a position where it can stay for a period of time, and leave it there.

vacation [veikéiʃən] n. 휴가, 방학; v. 휴가를 얻다 (paid vacation n. 유급 휴가)
A vacation is a period of time during which you relax and enjoy yourself away from home.

nod [nɑd] v. (고개를) 끄덕이다, 끄덕여 나타내다; n. (고개를) 끄덕임
If you nod, you move your head downward and upward to show agreement, understanding, or approval.

discuss [diskʌ́s] v. 토론하다, 논의하다, ~에 관하여 (서로) 이야기하다
If people discuss something, they talk about it, often in order to reach a decision.

coach [koutʃ] n. 코치; v. 코치하다, 지도하다
A coach is someone who trains a person or team of people in a particular sport.

pull together idiom (조직적으로 다툼 없이) 함께 일하다, 협력하다
If a group of people pull together, they act or work together in order to achieve something.

kink [kiŋk] n. (기계·계획 등의) 결함; (실·밧줄 등의) 꼬임, 비틀림; v. 꼬이다
A kink is a flaw or imperfection likely to hinder the successful operation of a machine or plan.

: normal [nɔ́:rməl] a. 보통의, 정상적인; n. 표준, 정상, 보통
Something that is normal is usual and ordinary, and is what people expect.

: suggest [səgdʒést] v. 제안하다; 암시하다
If you suggest something, you put forward a plan or idea for someone to think about.

. assistant [əsístənt] a. 보조의; n. 보조, 조수
Assistant is used in front of titles or jobs to indicate a slightly lower rank.

: fold [fould] v. (손·팔·다리를) 끼다, 포개다; 접다, 접어 포개다
If you fold your arms or hands, you bring them together and cross or link them, for example over your chest.

. dumb [dʌm] a. 멍청한, 우둔한; 벙어리의, 말을 하지 않는
If you say that something is dumb, you think that it is silly and annoying.

. stroke [strouk] ① v. 쓰다듬다, 어루만지다; n. 쓰다듬기, 달램 ② n. 타격, 일격, 치기
If you stroke someone or something, you move your hand slowly and gently over them.

: chin [tʃin] n. 턱
Your chin is the part of your face that is below your mouth and above your neck.

: natural [nǽtʃərəl] a. 당연한, 자연스러운; 자연의, 천연의
If you say that it is natural for someone to act in a particular way or for something to happen in that way, you mean that it is reasonable in the circumstances.

: concern [kənsə́:rn] v. 염려하다; ~에 관계하다; 관심을 갖다; n. 염려; 관심
If something concerns you, it worries you.

ᵇᵃafter all idiom 어쨌든; (예상과는 달리) 결국에는
You use after all when you are saying that something that you thought
might not be the case is in fact the case.

beyond [bijánd] prep. (범위·한도) ~을 넘어서; (시간) ~을 지나서; (장소) ~의 너머로
If something goes beyond a particular point or stage, it progresses or
increases so that it passes that point or stage.

consider [kənsídər] v. 고려하다, 숙고하다
If you consider something, you think about it carefully.

rub [rʌb] v. 비비다, 문지르다; 스치다; n. 문지르기
If you rub a part of your body, you move your hand or fingers backward
and forward over it while pressing firmly.

definite [défənit] a. 확실한, 확고한; 분명한, 뚜렷한 (definitely ad. 확실히, 명확히)
If something such as a decision or an arrangement is definite, it is firm
and clear, and unlikely to be changed.

ᵇᵃexact [igzǽkt] a. 정확한, 정밀한 (exactly ad. 정확하게, 꼭)
Exact means correct in every detail.

grin [grin] v. (이를 드러내고) 싱긋 웃다, 활짝 웃다; n. 싱긋 웃음
When you grin, you smile broadly.

broad [brɔːd] a. (폭이) 넓은; (빛이) 환한 (broadly ad. 활짝)
A broad smile is one in which your mouth is stretched very wide because
you are very pleased or amused.

promotion [prəmóuʃən] n. 승진, 승격; 진흥, 촉진
If you are given promotion or a promotion in your job, you are given a
more important job or rank in the organization that you work for.

suspicious [səspíʃəs] a. 의심하는, 수상쩍은 (suspiciously ad. 수상쩍은 듯이)
If you are suspicious of someone or something, you do not trust them,
and are careful when dealing with them.

tone [toun] n. (목)소리, 음성; 어조, 말씨; 색조

Someone's tone is a quality in their voice which shows what they are feeling or thinking.

odd [ad] a. 이상한, 기묘한

If you describe someone or something as odd, you think that they are strange or unusual.

be bound to idiom 반드시 ~하다, ~하게 마련이다

If you say that something is bound to happen or be true, you feel confident and certain of it.

Chapter 8

1. **What was Arthur doing in the garage?**

   A. He was throwing a baseball against the wall.

   B. He was throwing a tennis ball against the wall.

   C. He was throwing a rubber ball against the wall.

   D. He was throwing a basketball against the wall.

2. **Why did Arthur think that Francine had come to visit him?**

   A. He thought she came to make more insults.

   B. He thought she came to practice with him.

   C. He thought she came to ask him to try harder.

   D. He thought she came to borrow his baseball equipment.

3. Why did Francine really come to visit Arthur?

A. She came to ask Arthur to apologize to the team.

B. She came to insult Arthur for not playing well.

C. She came to help Arthur improve playing baseball.

D. She came to tell Arthur to join a new baseball team.

4. What advice did Francine tell Arthur to think about when catching the ball?

A. He should not use the glove to keep the sun out of his eyes.

B. He should think of doing everything at once.

C. He should think about breaking it into steps.

D. He should hold his arm low to keep his balance.

5. How did Arthur know how to help Francine with her fastball?

A. He had thought of the idea while watching a baseball game on TV.

B. He had heard D.W. explaining the idea to their mother.

C. He had asked D.W. for her advice about each member on the team.

D. He was a natural baseball genius.

Check Your Reading Speed

1분에 몇 단어를 읽는지 리딩 속도를 측정해보세요.

$$\frac{712 \ words}{reading \ time \ (\qquad) \ sec} \times 60 = (\qquad) \ WPM$$

Build Your Vocabulary

◦ **garage** [gərá:dʒ] n. 차고, 주차장
A garage is a building in which you keep a car.

복습 **bounce** [bauns] v. 튀다, 튀게 하다; 급히 움직이다, 뛰어다니다; n. 튐, 바운드
When an object such as a ball bounces or when you bounce it, it moves upward from a surface or away from it immediately after hitting it.

◦ **driveway** [dráivwèi] n. (도로에서 집·차고까지의) 진입로, 차도
A driveway is a piece of hard ground that leads from the road to the front of a house or other building.

‡ **ignore** [ignɔ́:r] v. 무시하다, 모르는 체하다
If you ignore someone or something, you pay no attention to them.

◦ **bet** [bet] v. 틀림없이 ~이다, 확신하다; 걸다, 내기를 하다; n. 내기, 건 돈
You use expressions such as 'I bet', 'I'll bet', and 'you can bet' to indicate that you are sure something is true.

think up idiom ~을 생각해 내다, 고안하다
If you think up an idea, a plan or a story, you create them in your mind.

◦ **insult** [insʌ́lt] n. 모욕(적인 말·행동); v. 모욕하다
An insult is a rude remark, or something a person says or does which insults you.

redden [redn] v. 빨개지다, 붉어지다
If someone reddens or their face reddens, their face turns pink or red, often because they are embarrassed or angry.

assistant [əsístənt] a. 보조의; n. 보조, 조수
Assistant is used in front of titles or jobs to indicate a slightly lower rank.

coach [koutʃ] n. 코치; v. 코치하다, 지도하다
A coach is someone who trains a person or team of people in a particular sport.

congratulate [kəngrǽtʃuleit] v. 축하하다 (congratulation n. 축하)
If you congratulate someone, you say something to show you are pleased that something nice has happened to them.

in charge of idiom ~을 맡고 있는, 담당의
If you have charge of or are in charge of something or someone, you have responsibility for them.

criticize [krítəsàiz] v. 비평하다, 비난하다 (criticism n. 비난)
If you criticize someone or something, you express your disapproval of them by saying what you think is wrong with them.

carry away idiom (흥분·열중한 나머지) 자신을 잊게 하다, 흥분시키다
If you are carried away, you lose self-control.

lately [léitli] ad. 요즘에, 최근에, 근래
You use lately to describe events in the recent past, or situations that started a short time ago.

cross [krɔːs] v. (서로) 교차하다, 엇갈리다; (가로질러) 건너다; n. X표, 십자가
If you cross your arms, legs, or fingers, you put one of them on top of the other.

tease [tiːz] v. 놀리다, 장난하다; n. 장난, 놀림
To tease someone means to laugh at them or make jokes about them in order to embarrass, annoy, or upset them.

embarrass [imbǽrəs] v. 부끄럽게[무안하게] 하다; 어리둥절하게 하다, 당황하다
(embarrassed a. 부끄러운)
If something or someone embarrasses you, they make you feel shy or ashamed.

sigh [sai] v. 한숨 쉬다; n. 한숨, 탄식
When you sigh, you let out a deep breath, as a way of expressing feelings such as disappointment, tiredness, or pleasure.

glove [glʌv] n. 장갑
Gloves are pieces of clothing which cover your hands and wrists and have individual sections for each finger.

backyard [bǽkjáːrd] n. 뒤뜰
A backyard is an area of land at the back of a house.

overhead [óuvərhéd] ad. 머리 위로, 하늘 높이
You use overhead to indicate that something is above you or above the place that you are talking about.

underneath [ʌ̀ndərníːθ] prep. ~의 밑에, 아래에; n. 밑면, 하부
If one thing is underneath another, it is directly under it, and may be covered or hidden by it.

land [lænd] v. (땅·표면에) 내려앉다, 착륙하다; n. 육지, 땅
When someone or something lands, they come down to the ground after moving through the air or falling.

smother [smʌ́ðəːr] v. 억제하다, 감추다; 숨막히게 하다, 숨을 막다
If you smother an emotion or a reaction, you control it so that people do not notice it.

giggle [gigl] n. 낄낄 웃음; v. 낄낄 웃다
A giggle is a sound or an action of laughing in a childlike way.

raise [reiz] v. 들어올리다, 들다; 키우다, 기르다
If you raise something, you move it so that it is in a higher position.

follow [fálou] v. 따라가다, 뒤따르다, ~의 뒤를 잇다

If you follow someone who is going somewhere, you move along behind them because you want to go to the same place.

path [pæθ] n. 길, 방향; 작은 길

The path of something is the line which it moves along in a particular direction.

blind [blaind] v. 눈멀게 하다; a. 눈먼, 장님인

If something blinds you, it makes you unable to see, either for a short time or permanently.

block [blak] v. (길 등을) 막다, 방해하다; n. 덩어리, 블록

To block a road, channel, or pipe means to put an object across it or in it so that nothing can pass through it or along it.

ouch [autʃ] int. 아야(갑자기 아파서 내지르는 소리)

'Ouch!' is used in writing to represent the noise that people make when they suddenly feel pain.

practice [præktis] v. 연습하다; 실행하다; n. 연습, 훈련; 실행, 실천

If you practice something, you keep doing it regularly in order to be able to do it better.

get the hang of ~ idiom ~의 사용법을 알다, 터득하다

If you get the hang of something, you learn or begin to understand how to do or use it.

advice [ædváis] n. 충고, 조언

If you give someone advice, you tell them what you think they should do in a particular situation.

pitch [pitʃ] v. 던지다; 처박다; n. 던지기, 투구; 경기장; 최고도, 정점

In the game of baseball or rounders, when you pitch the ball, you throw it to the batter for them to hit it.

crouch [krautʃ] v. 몸을 쭈그리다, 쪼그리고 앉다; 웅크리다; n. 웅크림

If you are crouching, your legs are bent under you so that you are close to the ground and leaning forward slightly.

stance [stæns] n. 자세, 스탠스
Your stance is the way that you are standing.

fire [faiər] v. 발사[발포]하다; 해고하다; n. 불, 화재
If someone fires a gun or a bullet, or if they fire, a bullet is sent from a gun that they are using.

sail [seil] v. 미끄러지듯 나아가다; 항해하다; n. 배의 돛; 항해, 보트타기
If a person or thing sails somewhere, they move there smoothly and fairly quickly.

fence [fens] n. 울타리, 담; v. 둘러막다
A fence is a barrier between two areas of land, made of wood or wire supported by posts.

position [pəzíʃən] n. 위치, 자세; 입장, 처지; v. (특정한 장소에) 두다
The position of someone or something is the place where they are in relation to other things.

release [rilí:s] v. 놓아주다, 해방시키다, 풀어놓다; n. 석방
If you release someone or something, you stop holding them.

follow through idiom 공을 따라가듯 팔을 끝까지 죽 돌리다
If you follow through, you complete a stroke by continuing to move the bat or club, after you have hit the ball.

explain [ikspléin] v. 설명하다, 분명하게 하다
If you explain something, you give details about it or describe it so that it can be understood.

shrug [ʃrʌg] v. (양 손바닥을 내보이면서 어깨를) 으쓱하다; n. (어깨를) 으쓱하기
If you shrug, you raise your shoulders to show that you are not interested in something or that you do not know or care about something.

especially [ispéʃəli] ad. 특히, 각별히
You use especially to emphasize that what you are saying applies more to one person, thing, or area than to any others.

70

please [pliːz] v. 기쁘게 하다, 즐겁게 하다 (pleased a. 기뻐하는, 만족해하는)
If you are pleased, you are happy about something or satisfied with something.

tip [tip] ① n. 조언, 힌트; 팁, 사례금 ② v. 뒤집어엎다, 기울이다 ③ n. (뾰족한) 끝
A tip is a useful piece of advice.

pause [pɔːz] v. 중단하다, 잠시 멈추다; n. 멈춤, 중지
If you pause while you are doing something, you stop for a short period and then continue.

nod [nad] v. (고개를) 끄덕이다, 끄덕여 나타내다; n. (고개를) 끄덕임
If you nod, you move your head downward and upward to show agreement, understanding, or approval.

overdo [òuvərdúː] v. 지나치게 하다, 과장하다
If someone overdoes something, they behave in an extreme way.

deal [diːl] v. 거래하다; 취급하다, 다루다; 분배하다; n. 거래, 계약
If you deal, you do business regularly with a person, an organization, or a government.

fault [fɔːlt] n. 과실, 잘못; 결점
If a bad or undesirable situation is your fault, you caused it or are responsible for it.

figure [fígjər] v. 생각하다, 판단하다; 계산하다; n. 형태, 형상; 수치, 숫자
If you figure that something is the case, you think or guess that it is the case.

neighborhood [néibərhùd] n. 근처, 이웃; 이웃 사람들
The neighborhood of a place or person is the area or the people around them.

freeze [friːz] v. (froze–frozen) (두려움 등으로 몸이) 얼어붙다; 얼다, 얼리다
If someone who is moving freezes, they suddenly stop and become completely still and quiet.

Chapter 9

1. **Who did the Eagles face in their first game?**

   A. The Penguins

   B. The Poodles

   C. The Roosters

   D. The Polar Bears

2. **How did D.W. feel about Arthur playing?**

   A. She was embarrassed to be his sister.

   B. She said she taught him everything he knew.

   C. She said she wanted to be just like him.

   D. She was worried that he might get injured.

3. How did Buster do when he batted?

A. He made a hit and run to first base.

B. He walked to first base.

C. He hit a home run.

D. He struck out.

4. What did the Brain do before pitching?

A. He licked his finger and checked the wind direction.

B. He breathed slowly and relaxed his mind.

C. He closed his eyes and thought of his pitch.

D. He made a signal to the umpire.

5. What happened to the deep fly ball headed for Arthur?

A. It hit Arthur in the head.

B. It landed in a storm drain.

C. It landed in Arthur's glove.

D. It went over the fence.

Check Your Reading Speed

1분에 몇 단어를 읽는지 리딩 속도를 측정해보세요.

$$\frac{428 \text{ words}}{\text{reading time (} \quad \text{) sec}} \times 60 = (\quad) \text{ WPM}$$

Build Your Vocabulary

coach [kouʧ] n. 코치; v. 코치하다, 지도하다

A coach is someone who trains a person or team of people in a particular sport.

pace [peis] v. 서성거리다; (일의) 속도를 유지하다; n. 속도

If you pace a small area, you keep walking up and down it, because you are anxious or impatient.

back and forth idiom 앞뒤로, 좌우로

If someone moves back and forth, they repeatedly move in one direction and then in the opposite direction.

breath [breθ] n. 숨, 호흡 (take a deep breath idiom 심호흡하다)

Your breath is the air that you let out through your mouth when you breathe.

practice [præktis] n. 연습, 훈련; 실행, 실천; v. 연습하다; 실행하다

Practice means doing something regularly in order to be able to do it better.

clap [klæp] v. 박수를 치다; n. 박수 (소리)

When you clap, you hit your hands together to show appreciation or attract attention.

field [fi:ld] n. 수비; 경기장, 구장; 들, 들판; v. (공을) 잡다

If your team takes the field, the team is in the field, as opposed to the one at bat.

sharp [ʃɑːrp] a. (커브 등이) 급격한; (칼날 등이) 날카로운 (sharply ad. 급격히)
A sharp bend or turn is one that changes direction suddenly.

base [beis] n. [야구] −루, 베이스; 기초, 근거, 토대 (second base n. 2루)
A base in baseball, softball, or rounders is one of the places at each corner of the square on the pitch.

cheer [tʃiər] v. 환호성을 지르다, 응원하다; n. 환호(성)
When people cheer, they shout loudly to show their approval or to encourage someone who is doing something such as taking part in a game.

bleacher [bliːtʃər] n. (pl.) (지붕 없는) 야외 관람석
The bleachers are a part of an outdoor sports stadium, or the seats in that area, which are usually uncovered and are the least expensive place where people can sit.

run [rʌn] n. [야구] 득점; 뛰기, 달리기; v. 뛰다, 달리다; 경영하다
In cricket or baseball, a run is a score of one, which is made by players running between marked places on the field after hitting the ball.

bat [bæt] ① v. (야구·크리켓에서 배트로) 공을 치다; n. 방망이, 배트 ② n. 박쥐
When you bat, you have a turn at hitting the ball with a bat in baseball, softball, cricket, or rounders.

rap [ræp] v. 쾅쾅[똑똑] 두드리다, 가볍게 치다
If you rap on something or rap it, you hit or strike it with a quick or light blow.

way to go idiom 잘했어
People say 'way to go!' to encourage someone to continue the good work.

yell [jel] v. 소리치다, 고함치다; n. 고함소리, 부르짖음
If you yell, you shout loudly, usually because you are excited, angry, or in pain.

foul [faul] v. 파울로 치다, 파울을 범하다; a. 규칙 위반인; (성격·맛 등이) 아주 안 좋은

In a game or sport, if a player fouls another player, they touch them or block them in a way which is not allowed according to the rules.

pitch [pitʃ] n. 던지기, 투구; 경기장; 최고도, 정점; v. 던지다; 처박다

In baseball, a pitch is the act of throwing a baseball by a pitcher to a batter.

swing [swiŋ] v. (swung–swung) 휘두르다, (한 점을 축으로 하여) 빙 돌다, 휙 움직이다

If something swings in a particular direction or if you swing it in that direction, it moves in that direction with a smooth, curving movement.

all the way idiom 완전히; 내내, 줄곧

All the way means completely.

umpire [ʌ́mpaiər] n. (테니스·야구 경기 등의) 심판; v. 심판을 보다

An umpire is a person whose job is to make sure that a sports match or contest is played fairly and that the rules are not broken.

stand [stænd] n. 관람석; 가판대, 좌판; v. 서다, 일어서다; 참다, 견디다

A stand at a sports ground is a large structure where people sit or stand to watch what is happening.

scoreless [skɔ́:rlis] a. (양팀 모두) 득점 없는

In football, baseball, and some other sports, a scoreless game is one in which neither team has scored any goals or points.

lead [li:d] ① n. 선도, 지휘; v. 이끌다, 인솔하다 ② n. [광물] 납

If you have the lead or are in the lead in a race or competition, you are winning.

batter [bǽtər] ① n. 타자 ② v. 난타하다, 강타하다

In sports such as baseball and softball, a batter is a person who hits the ball with a wooden bat.

lick [lik] v. 핥다; n. 한 번 핥기, 핥아먹기

When people or animals lick something, they move their tongue across its surface.

direction [dirékʃən] n. 방향; 지도, 지시
A direction is the general line that someone or something is moving or pointing in.

thwack [θwæk] n. 찰싹 때리는 소리; v. 찰싹 때리다
A thwack is a sound made when two solid objects hit each other hard.

backpedal [bǽkpedl] v. 뒷걸음질치다; 자전거의 페달을 거꾸로 밟아 속도를 늦추다
If you backpedal, you step backward.

grass [græs] n. 풀밭, 초원; 풀
If you talk about the grass, you are referring to an area of ground that is covered with grass, for example in your garden.

blink [bliŋk] v. 눈을 깜박거리다; (등불·별 등이) 깜박이다; n. 깜박거림
When you blink or when you blink your eyes, you shut your eyes and very quickly open them again.

shield [ʃiːld] v. 막다, 지키다, 보호하다; n. 방패
If something or someone shields you from a danger or risk, they protect you from it.

fence [fens] n. 울타리, 담; v. 둘러막다
A fence is a barrier between two areas of land, made of wood or wire supported by posts.

plop [plap] n. 퐁당 (하는 소리); v. 털썩 주저앉다; 퐁당[툭] 하고 떨어지다
A plop is a soft, gentle sound, like the sound made by something dropping into water without disturbing the surface much.

relay [ríːlei] v. (정보·뉴스 등을 받아서) 전달하다; 교대시키다; n. 릴레이 경주; 교대
If you relay something that has been said to you, you repeat it to another person.

spin [spin] v. (spun–spun) (빙빙) 돌다; (이야기를) 만들어 내다; n. 회전
If someone spins around, they turn very quickly to face in the opposite direction.

‡ plant [plænt] v. (지면 등에) 놓다, 든든하게 세우다; (나무·씨앗 등을) 심다;
n. 식물, 초목; 공장
If you plant something somewhere, you put it there firmly.

복습 firm [fə:rm] ① a. 굳은, 단단한; 견고한 (firmly ad. 굳게) ② n. 회사
If something is firm, it does not shake or move when you put weight or
pressure on it, because it is strongly made or securely fastened.

복습 fire [faiər] v. 발사[발포]하다; 해고하다; n. 불, 화재
If someone fires a gun or a bullet, or if they fire, a bullet is sent from a
gun that they are using.

＊ slide [slaid] v. 미끄러지다, 미끄러지듯 움직이다
If you slide somewhere, you move there smoothly and quietly.

‡ sweep [swi:p] v. (swept-swept) (거칠게) 휩쓸고 가다; (빗자루·손 등으로) 쓸다
If you sweep things off something, you push them off with a quick
smooth movement of your arm.

복습 trot [trat] v. 빠른 걸음으로 가다; 총총걸음 치다; n. 빠른 걸음
If you trot somewhere, you move fairly fast at a speed between walking
and running, taking small quick steps.

복습 turn [tə:rn] n. 차례, 순번; 회전; 방향전환; v. 돌리다, 회전하다, 뒤엎다
If it is your turn to do something, you now have the duty, chance, or right
to do it, when other people have done it before you or will do it after you.

Chapter 10

1. **What did the coach say of the game after Sue Ellen batted?**

   A. He said that they were going to lose the game.

   B. He said that the tieing run was on first.

   C. He said that Sue Ellen should bat again.

   D. He said that Sue Ellen could have hit a home run.

2. **What happened when Binky was at bat?**

   A. He missed the ball when he swung.

   B. He hit a ball and ran to first base.

   C. He hit a ball, but it was caught.

   D. He hit a ground ball.

3. What did the team need Buster to do?

A. They needed Buster to guard home plate.

B. They needed Buster to make a single.

C. They needed Buster to strike out.

D. They needed Buster to let someone else bat.

4. What did Arthur, Francine, and Buster decide to do immediately after the game?

A. They decided to practice more right there on the field.

B. They decided to go home and watch baseball games on TV.

C. They decided to go to the Sugar Bowl to celebrate.

D. They decided to quit playing baseball on the Eagles team.

5. What did Francine thank Arthur for in the end?

A. She thanked him for letting her tease Arthur.

B. She thanked him for helping the Eagles win their first game.

C. She thanked him for playing on the Eagle team with her.

D. She thanked him for stopping her before she teased Buster.

Check Your Reading Speed

1분에 몇 단어를 읽는지 리딩 속도를 측정해보세요.

$$\frac{582 \text{ words}}{\text{reading time ( ) sec}} \times 60 = (\quad) \text{ WPM}$$

Build Your Vocabulary

field [fiːld] n. 경기장, 구장; 수비; 들, 들판; v. (공을) 잡다
A sports field is an area of grass where sports are played.

pitch [pitʃ] n. 던지기, 투구; 경기장; 최고도, 정점; v. 던지다; 처박다
In baseball, a pitch is the act of throwing a baseball by a pitcher to a batter.

nod [nad] v. (고개를) 끄덕이다, 끄덕여 나타내다; n. (고개를) 끄덕임
If you nod, you move your head downward and upward to show agreement, understanding, or approval.

batter [bǽtər] ① n. 타자 (batter's box n. 타자석) ② v. 난타하다, 강타하다
In sports such as baseball and softball, a batter is a person who hits the ball with a wooden bat.

swing [swiŋ] v. (swung–swung) 휘두르다, (한 점을 축으로 하여) 빙 돌다, 휙 움직이다
If something swings in a particular direction or if you swing it in that direction, it moves in that direction with a smooth, curving movement.

coach [koutʃ] n. 코치; v. 코치하다, 지도하다
A coach is someone who trains a person or team of people in a particular sport.

whistle [hwisl] v. 휘파람 불다; n. 휘파람; 호각
When someone whistles, they make a sound by forcing their breath out between their lips or their teeth.

tie [tai] v. (경기 등에서) 동점이 되다; 매다, 매듭을 짓다

If two people tie in a competition or game or if they tie with each other, they have the same number of points or the same degree of success.

advance [ædvǽns] v. 전진시키다, 나아가다; 진보하다

To advance means to move forward, often in order to attack someone.

tap [tæp] ① v. 톡톡 두드리다, 치다 ② n. 수도꼭지

If you tap something, you hit it with a quick light blow or a series of quick light blows.

dirt [dəːrt] n. 흙, 진흙, 먼지; 쓰레기

You can refer to the earth on the ground as dirt, especially when it is dusty.

cleat [kliːt] n. (구두 밑창의) 미끄럼막이; (선박의) 밧줄 걸이

A cleat is a metal or leather projection from the sole of a shoe for preventing slipping.

cock [kak] v. 위로 치올리다; (귀·꽁지를) 쫑긋 세우다; n. 수탉; 마개

If you cock a something in a particular direction, you lift it or point it in that direction.

bat [bæt] ① n. 방망이, 배트; v. (야구·크리켓에서 배트로) 공을 치다 ② n. 박쥐

A bat is a specially shaped piece of wood that is used for hitting the ball in baseball, softball, cricket, rounders, or table tennis.

fence [fens] n. 울타리, 담; v. 둘러막다

A fence is a barrier between two areas of land, made of wood or wire supported by posts.

contact [kántækt] n. 접촉; v. 접촉하다, 연락하다

When people or things are in contact, they are touching each other.

pop [pap] v. 불쑥 나타나다; 뻥 하고 터뜨리다; n. 뻥[탁] 하는 소리; 발포

If something pops up, it appears or happens when you do not expect it.

pitcher [pítʃər] ① n. 투수, 피처 ② n. 물 주전자
In baseball, the pitcher is the person who throws the ball to the batter, who tries to hit it.

breath [breθ] n. 숨, 호흡
Your breath is the air that you let out through your mouth when you breathe.

trip [trip] v. 걸려 넘어지다; 경쾌한 걸음걸이로 걷다; n. 여행
If you trip when you are walking, you knock your foot against something and fall or nearly fall.

grass [græs] n. 풀밭, 초원; 풀
If you talk about the grass, you are referring to an area of ground that is covered with grass, for example in your garden.

blind [blaind] v. 눈멀게 하다; a. 눈먼, 장님인
If something blinds you, it makes you unable to see, either for a short time or permanently.

itch [itʃ] n. 가려움; v. 가렵다, 근질근질하다
An itch is an uncomfortable feeling on your skin that makes you want to rub it with your nails.

scratch [skrætʃ] v. 긁다, 할퀴다; n. 생채기, 할큄, 찰과상
If you scratch yourself, you rub your fingernails against your skin because it is itching.

glove [glʌv] n. 장갑
Gloves are pieces of clothing which cover your hands and wrists and have individual sections for each finger.

thump [θʌmp] n. 탁[쿵] 하는 소리; 때림, 세게 쥐어박음; v. 탁 치다, 부딪치다
A thump is a loud, dull sound by hitting something.

trudge [trʌdʒ] v. 터벅터벅 걷다; n. 터덕터덕 걸음
If you trudge somewhere, you walk there slowly and with heavy steps, especially because you are tired or unhappy.

dugout [dʌ́gaut] n. (축구장·야구장의) 선수 대기석
A dugout is a shelter where players and coaches sit during sports games.

cheer [ʧiər] v. 환호성을 지르다, 응원하다; n. 환호(성)
When people cheer, they shout loudly to show their approval or to encourage someone who is doing something such as taking part in a game.

victory [víktəri] n. 승리, 우승
A victory is a success in a struggle, war, or competition.

effort [éfərt] n. 노력, 수고
If you make an effort to do something, you try very hard to do it.

storm [stɔːrm] v. 돌진하다; 격노하다; n. 폭풍우
If you storm into or out of a place, you enter or leave it quickly and noisily, because you are angry.

cough [kɔːf] v. 기침하다; n. 기침
When you cough, you force air out of your throat with a sudden, harsh noise. You often cough when you are ill, or when you are nervous or want to attract someone's attention.

pat [pæt] v. 톡톡 가볍게 치다, (애정을 담아) 쓰다듬다; n. 쓰다듬기
If you pat something or someone, you tap them lightly, usually with your hand held flat.

gather [gǽðər] v. 모이다, 집결하다; 모으다, 끌다
If people gather somewhere or if someone gathers people somewhere, they come together in a group.

replay [riːpléi] v. 재연하다; 재생하다; n. 재경기
If you replay an event in your mind, you think about it again and again.

shrug [ʃrʌg] v. (양 손바닥을 내보이면서 어깨를) 으쓱하다; n. (어깨를) 으쓱하기
If you shrug, you raise your shoulders to show that you are not interested in something or that you do not know or care about something.

tip [tip] ① n. 조언, 힌트; 팁, 사례금 ② v. 뒤집어엎다, 기울이다 ③ n. (뾰족한) 끝
A tip is a useful piece of advice.

brighten [braitn] v. 밝아지다; 빛나게 하다, 밝게 하다
If someone brightens or their face brightens, they suddenly look happier.

get together idiom (~와) 만나다; ~을 모으다
If people get together, they meet with someone for social purposes or to discuss or organize something.

empty [émpti] a. 빈, 공허한; v. 비우다
An empty place, vehicle, or container is one that has no people or things in it.

grab [græb] v. 부여잡다, 움켜쥐다; n. 부여잡기
If you grab something, you take it or pick it up suddenly and roughly.

whisper [hwíspər] v. 속삭이다; n. 속삭임
When you whisper, you say something very quietly.

tease [ti:z] v. 놀리다, 장난하다; n. 장난, 놀림
To tease someone means to laugh at them or make jokes about them in order to embarrass, annoy, or upset them.

stink [stiŋk] v. 몹시 나쁘다; (고약한) 냄새가 나다, 악취가 풍기다; n. 악취
To stink means to be extremely bad in quality or in one's performance.

pitcher [pítʃər] ① n. 투수, 피처 ② n. 물 주전자
In baseball, the pitcher is the person who throws the ball to the batter, who tries to hit it.

attention [əténʃən] n. 주의, 관심; 배려
If you give someone or something your attention, you look at it, listen to it, or think about it carefully.

definite [défənit] a. 확실한, 확고한; 분명한, 뚜렷한 (definitely ad. 확실히, 명확히)
If something such as a decision or an arrangement is definite, it is firm and clear, and unlikely to be changed.

1장

page 5

버스터와 아서는 야구 글러브를 들고 인도를 걷고 있었습니다. 그들은 걸으면서, 공을 던져 앞뒤로 주고받았습니다.

"그래서, 너 야구를 잘할 것 같아?" 버스터가 물었습니다.

아서는 어깨를 으쓱했습니다. "그러길 바라." 그가 말했습니다. 그는 긴장했다고 인정하고 싶지 않았습니다. 그는 작년에 다른 아이들이 했던 것처럼 야구를 하지 않았습니다.

"너 작년에 많이 배웠어?" 그가 물었습니다.

버스터는 웃었습니다. "많이 배웠냐고? 내가 한번 보여 줄게. 멀리 던지는 걸 잡을 수 있도록 뛰어가 봐."

page 6

아서는 나무를 지나서 걸어갔습니다.

버스터가 그에게 손짓했습니다. "더 멀리... 더 멀리... 좋아, 거기 서. 준비됐어? 네가 그 유명한 버스터 볼을 잡을 수 있는지 보자."

"준비됐어!" 아서가 말했습니다. 그는 글러브를 들어 올렸습니다.

버스터는 그가 할 수 있는 한 가장 세게 공을 던졌습니다. 하지만 공은 아서에게로 가는 대신 나무로 날아갔습니다. 그것은 가지 사이에서 이리저리 튀었습니다.

"내가 잡을게." 아서가 아래를 돌며 말했습니다.

공은 한 가지에서 튀어, 다른 가지로 가고, 지붕 위로 굴렀습니다.

"내가 아직 잡을 수 있어." 아서가 공의 모든 움직임을 쫓으며 말했습니다.

공은 지붕 아래로 굴러 홈통으로 들어갔습니다. 그것은 세로 홈통 밑으로 떨어져, 아서의 다리 사이를 지나, 빗물 배수구로 굴러갔습니다.

"이런!" 아서가 말했습니다. "결국 못 잡게 된 것 같네."

page 7

버스터는 배수구를 내려다보았습니다. 그는 한숨 쉬었습니다. "난 그런 식으로 공을 많이 잃어버려."

"너 잘 던지던데." 아서가 말했습니다. "너 그걸 단지 한 시즌 만에 배운 거야?"

"당연하지. 걱정해 마, 너도 금방 따라잡을 거야. 생각해 봐. 넌 경기장 한복판에 서 있어. 주위에는 아무도 없어."

"아무도 없어." 아서가 말했습니다.

"숨을 곳도 없어." 버스터가 말했습니다.

"숨을 곳도 없어." 아서가 따라했습니다.

"야구 방망이의 타격음과 함께, 공이 너를 향해 오고 있어. 모두가 쳐다보고 있어. 너의 모든 동작을 보면서 말이지."

"내 모든 동작을?" 아서가 말했습니다.

"당연하지." 버스터가 말했습니다. "그리고 단지 너의 팀원들뿐만 아니야. 상대팀도 보고 있어. 그리고 관중석에 있는 관중들도. 특히 너의 가족이."

page 8

"우리 가족?"

버스터는 고개를 끄덕였습니다. "그럼. 부모님. 조부모님. 형제들. 모두 경기장에 오잖아."

아서는 한숨 쉬었습니다. "내가 이걸 정리해 볼게. 그러니까 나는 경기장 한복판에 홀로 서 있고, 공이 나에게 올 때마다 온 세상이 나를 지켜보고 있다는 거야."

"정말 흥분되겠지?" 버스터가 말했습니다.

"그러게." 아서가 말했습니다. 사실 흥분은 그의 마음속에 있는 단어가 아니었습니다.

"그리고 타격도 잊지 마." 버스터가 말했습니다.

"나도 그러고 싶지는 않아."

버스터는 몸을 낮춰 타격 자세를 취했습니다. "단지 너와 투수뿐이야. 나머지는 중요하지 않아. 방망이를 들어. 준비해. 기다려. 공이 불을 뿜으며 날아와. 공이 지나갈 때 넌 열기를 느낄 수 있어."

아서는 마른침을 삼켰습니다. "열기를 느낀다고?"

"뭐, 아마도 아니겠지." 버스터가 인정했습니다. "그래도 그것은 긴장되는 순간이야."

page 10

"왜냐하면 모두가 보고 있으니까."

"바로 그거야. 심판이 말해, '스트라이크!' 하지만 괜찮아. 네가 노리던 공이 아니었어. 하지만 이제 넌 바짝 붙어 서."

"붙어 서." 아서가 말했습니다.

"또다시 속구야. 하지만 이번에는 네가 휘둘러. 공은 로켓처럼 쏜살같이 날아가. 홈런이야! 너는 베이스를 돌아서 환호하는 관중에게 가."

"그렇게 쉽게?" 아서가 말했습니다.

"뭐, 매번은 아니지만. 네가 운이 좋다면 그게 일어날 수도 있지."

아서가 한숨 쉬었습니다. 그는 그런 일이 자신에게 일어날지 알 수 없었습니다. 그래도 그렇게 생각해 보는 것은 좋았습니다.

2장

page 11

야구장에서, 한 무리의 아이들이 게시판 주위에서 팀 명단을 보면서 옹기종기 서 있었습니다.

"나 내 이름 찾았어." 버스터가 말했습니다. "어디 보자... 프랜신... 브레인... 빙키... 아서. 좋아! 좋아! 우리 모두 이글스야. 와, 우린 대단한 팀이 될 거야. 난 얼른 공을 던지고 싶어."

"이봐, 나도 던지고 싶어!" 프랜신이 말했습니다.

"나도 그래." 브레인이 말했습니다.

"우리 어떻게 정하지?" 버스터가 말했습니다.

"걱정하지 마." 프랜신이 말했습니다. "코치님이 정하실 거야."

page 12

"하지만 프랜신," 브레인이 말했습니다. "너희 아빠가 코치님이잖아."

그녀는 미소 지었습니다. "상황이 재미있게 돌아가네."

"뭐가 어떻게 돌아간다고?" 그녀의 아빠가 나타나 그들과 합류하며 말했습니다. 그는 이글스의 공식 티셔츠와 모자를 쓰고 있었습니다.

"아무것도 아니에요, 아빠." 프랜신이 그를 향해 미소 지으며 말했습니다.

"나 토할 것 같아." 버스터가 속삭였습니다.

"같이 토할 사람이 생긴 것 같은데. 나도 동감이야." 브레인이 속삭이며 대답했습니다.

수 엘렌, 스피디, 펀, 그리고 알렉스를 포함한 모든 팀원들이 잔디밭에 앉았습니다.

"우리의 첫 연습에 모두들 이렇게 와줘서 기쁘구나." 코치님이 말했습니다. "대부분이 알고 있듯이, 나는 올리버 프렌스키이고, 프랜신의 아빠야."

page 13

프랜신은 버스터를 보고 활짝 웃었습니다.

"이제, 우리의 모토는 '팀워크'야!" 코치님은 계속했습니다. "만약 여러분이 좋아하는 포지션이 있다면, 그것으로 시작해도 좋아. 하지만, 모두들 돌아가며 하게 될 거야. 누가 제일 먼저 투수를 해볼까?"

버스터, 프랜신, 그리고 브레인이 모두 손을 들었습니다.

"훌륭해. 지원자가 많구나. 버스터, 네가 처음으로 하지 않을래?"

"그치만.. 그치만—" 프랜신이 더듬거리며 말했습니다.

"네 순서가 있을 거야." 그녀의 아빠가 그녀를 안심시켰습니다.

다른 모두가 포지션을 취했습니다. 아서는 결국 오른쪽 외야에 가게 되었습니다. 아무도 거기에 있고 싶지 않은 것처럼 보였습니다.

"모두들 고개를 들어!" 코치님이 홈플레이트에서 야구 방망이를 들고 기다리며 말했습니다. "시작해 봐, 버스터."

버스터는 공을 던질 준비를 했습니다. 그는 팔을 돌리고, 다리를 뻗고, 그가 할 수 있는 한 가장 세게 공을 던졌습니다.

프렌스키 코치님은 눈을 깜박거렸습니다.

"공이 어디로 갔지?"

버스터는 확신할 수 없었습니다. 그는 버스터 볼에 있어서는 절대 확신할 수 없었습니다. 잠시 후 공이 내려와 그의 머리를 쳤습니다.

"너 괜찮니, 버스터?" 코치님이 물었습니다.

버스터는 고개를 끄덕였습니다.

"좋아. 다시 해보자. 하지만 이번에는 힘을 좀 빼자. 첫날에 팔을 고장 내지는 말자고."

버스터는 고개를 끄덕였습니다. 그가 다시 공을 던졌습니다. 그리고 공은 홈 플레이트 바로 위로 날아왔습니다. 코치님은 3루에 있는 수 엘렌에게 직선타를 날렸습니다.

몇 번의 투구 후에, 이제 프랜신의 차례였습니다. 그녀가 처음 던진 공들은 높고 스트라이크존 밖으로 빠졌습니다. 그녀의 아빠는 그것들을 파울 타구로 쳐냈습니다.

"힘이 넘치는데." 그가 말했습니다.

"이제 기억해, 홈 플레이트 바로 위로."

프랜신의 다음 투구들은 나아졌습니다. 그녀의 아빠는 그것들을 경기장 여러 군데로 쳤습니다.

내 속구가 나올 시간이야, 프랜신은 생각했습니다.

그녀는 공을 세게 잡고 던졌습니다.

공은 모든 것 위로 날아갔습니다. 그녀의 아빠, 빙키, 심지어 그물망까지 말이죠.

"뭐," 그녀의 아빠가 말했습니다. "확실히 홈 플레이트 위로 들어오긴 했네."

"너무 위였죠." 빙키가 말했습니다.

코치님은 목을 가다듬었습니다. "좋아, 프랜신, 다른 사람에게 기회를 주자꾸나."

브레인이 마운드로 왔습니다.

"준비됐니?" 코치님이 물었습니다.

"잠깐만요." 브레인이 말했습니다. 그는 손가락을 핥은 다음 위로 들어 바람의 방향을 시험했습니다. 그러더니 그는 마운드를 운동화로 긁기 시작했습니다.

"다 괜찮은 거니?" 코치님이 물었습니다.

"아, 그럼요." 브레인이 말했습니다. "발을 제대로 딛는 건 매우 중요하잖아요."

마침내 그가 준비되었을 때, 브레인은 조심스럽게 그의 첫 투구를 했습니다.

프렌스키 코치님은 유격수 쪽으로 땅볼을 쳤습니다.

브레인은 만족했습니다. 그는 바람과 발 디딤을 다시 점검했습니다. 그는 매 투구마다 그렇게 해서, 많이 던질 수 없었습니다.

마지막 공은 경기장의 오른쪽으로 갔습니다. 그것은 아주 높이 뜬 공이었습니다.

"내가 잡을게!" 아서가 뒤로 움직이며 말했습니다. 그는 그가 적절한 순간이라고 생각했을 때 뛰어올랐습니다.

page 18

그리고 놓쳤습니다.

공은 그의 뒤로 내려왔습니다.

"거의 다 잡았는데!" 코치님이 말했습니다. "아서, 아주 우아한 점프였어."

우아한? 아서는 우아하게 느껴지지 않았습니다. 그는 자신의 얼굴이 붉어지는 것을 느낄 수 있었습니다. 그는 모두가 자신을 보고 있다는 것을 알았습니다.

아무래도 이 시즌이 매우 긴 시즌이 될 것처럼 보이기 시작했습니다.

3장

page 19

아서는 그의 침실 거울 앞에 서서, 공을 위아래로 던지며 글러브로 받았습니다.

아빠가 복도에 서서 그를 쳐다보았습니다. "다음 연습할 준비됐니, 아서?" 그가 물었습니다.

아서는 공을 놓쳤습니다. "어, 어... 네." 그가 말했습니다.

리드 씨는 방안으로 들어왔습니다. "다 괜찮은 거지?"

"음, 아마도요. 연습이 힘들었어요."

"정말? 그것에 대해서 나한테 말해보렴."

"전 아직 편하지가 않아요. 지난번에는 2루수를 맡았어요. 날카로운 땅볼을 잡았는데, 공을 글러브에서 빼지 못했어요. 공이 마치 풀로 붙어 있는 것 같았죠."

page 20

"어떻게 했니?" 아빠가 물었습니다.

"그게, 2루에서 공을 달라고 강요했어요. 그래서 글러브를 벗어서 2루를 밟고 있던 유격수에게 던졌죠."

"제때에 던졌니?"

아서는 한숨 쉬었습니다. "글러브는 그랬죠. 하지만 공은 도중에 나와서 외야로 굴러갔어요. 주자는 결국 3루로 갔죠."

"코치님은 뭐라고 하셨니?" 리드 씨가 물었습니다.

"제가 기발하다고 하셨어요. 매우 창

의적이라고요. 그는 제가 경기할 때 그런 단어들을 매우 많이 쓰세요."

리드 씨는 침대 위에 앉았습니다. "코치님이 좋은 눈을 가지고 계시는구나, 아서. 넌 단지 시간을 좀 더 들여야 할 뿐이야."

page 21

아서는 확신이 들지 않았습니다. "다른 모두는 저보다 훨씬 앞서 가고 있는 것 같아요. 그리고 저는 다른 모두가 이미 다 알고 있는 것들을 도와달라고 말하는 것이 우습게 느껴져요."

"그래, 음, 다른 아이들은 대부분 작년에 야구를 했지만, 넌 안 했지. 먼저 시작하는 것은 차이점을 만든단다. 나도 그런 적이 있었지."

"아빠도요?"

아빠는 고개를 끄덕였습니다. "그건 내가 요리에 처음 흥미를 가졌을 때야. 물론, 그때는 내가 음식 출장 서비스 사업을 하게 될지 몰랐었어. 나는 그저 음식을 가지고 실험하는 것이 좋았어. 난 첫 주에 아파서 선생님이 모든 기구가 작동하는 법을 알려주는 수업을 놓쳤단다. 그 다음 주에 나는 너무 쑥스러워 질문하지 못했지. 난 그저 다른 사람들이 아는 만큼 알고 있는 척했어."

page 23

"그게 먹혔나요?" 아서가 물었습니다.

아빠는 미소 지었습니다. "몇 분 동안은 그랬지. 하지만 우리는 믹서로 샐러드 소스를 만들어야 했어. 다른 사람들은 뚜껑이 특정한 방법으로 잠겨야 한다는 것을 알았지만 나는 아니었지. 그래서 내가 그것을 켜니까..."

아서는 헉 하는 소리를 냈습니다.

"네가 짐작한 대로야. 샐러드 소스는 결국 온 사방으로 모든 사람한테 튀었지. 정말 난장판이었어."

"아빠는 난처해졌나요?"

아빠는 얼굴을 찡그렸습니다. "잠시 동안 나는 내 인생이 끝났다고 생각했어. 선생님은 끈적거리는 소스를 뒤집어쓰고 있었지. 그는 나에게 주먹을 흔들었고, 소스는 그의 손에서 떨어져 바닥으로 떨어졌지."

아서의 입이 떡 벌어졌습니다.

"교실은 완전히 정적에 휩싸였어. 그러다 선생님이 웃기 시작했지. '이것이,' 그가 말했어, '우리가 *지난주*에 얘기했던 것의 좋은 예입니다.'"

page 24

아서는 한숨 쉬었습니다. "그래서 살아남았군요."

"맞아. 하지만 나는 다시는 내가 하는 것에 대해 알고 있는 척하려고 하지 않았어. 그리고 너도 그러면 안 된단다. 도움이나 조언을 요청하는 것을 두려워하지 마. 너는 머지 않아 따라잡을 수 있을 거야."

page 25

프렌스키 코치님은 그의 팀이 준비 운동을 하는 것을 보면서, 그물망 뒤에 서 있었습니다.

"실례합니다. 코치님?"

코치님이 몸을 돌렸습니다.

"저는 버스터의 엄마 빗시예요."

"만나서 반갑습니다. 버스터는 참 괜찮은 아이예요. 늘 주도적이죠!"

"그렇게 말씀해 주시니 감사하네요. 저 그냥 궁금한 게 있는데... 공이 매우 단단하나요?"

"음, 다른 야구공보다 더 단단하진 않죠."

"그렇군요. 저 그냥 궁금해서 그러는데... 만약 그게 버스터를 맞추면 어떡하죠?"

page 26

"음, 항상 약간의 위험은 있지만 버스터는 매우 빨라요. 제가 확신하건대—"

"그리고 야구모자 말이에요. 그게 모직물로 만들어졌나요? 제 생각에 버스터는 모직물에 알레르기가 있어요. 만약 버스터가 긁기 시작한다면, 경기에 최선을 다할 수 있을 것 같지 않아요."

"버스터가 긁는지 모두가 주시하겠습니다." 프렌스키 코치님은 관람석을 힐끗 쳐다보았습니다. "자, 이제 자리를 찾으시라고 권해드리고 싶네요. 음, 빗시. 좋은 자리를 다 뺏기고 싶지는 않겠죠?"

"연습 때도 자리가 다 차나요?"

프렌스키 코치님은 망설였습니다. "어떻게 될지는 알 수 없죠." 그가 말했습니다.

경기장에서, 아서와 버스터는 공을 서로에게 던지고 있었습니다. 프랜신이 다가오자, 버스터는 상상의 마이크를 그녀 입 앞에 갖다 댔습니다.

"실례합니다, 강타자님. 액션 뉴스의 버스터입니다. 오늘 본인의 기록인 49개의 높이 뜬 공을 깰 수 있을 것 같나요?"

page 27

"아주 웃기네." 프랜신이 말했습니다. "적어도 내가 던지면 홈 플레이트 위로 가기라도 하지."

"진정해." 아서가 말했습니다. "너희 둘 다 같은 팀이야, 기억해?"

"여기서 빠져, 아서." 프랜신이 말했습니다. "넌 공을 잡는 데나 네 모든 주의를 집중해."

"오, 그렇단 말이지?" 아서는 손을 엉덩이에 갖다 대었고, 공이 그의 글러브에서 떨어졌습니다.

프랜신은 소리내어 웃고는 경기장으로 움직였습니다.

"네가 필요한 게 뭔 줄 알아, 아서?"

버스터가 말했습니다. "나의 절대 실패하지 않는, 늘 성공하는, 100퍼센트 보장된, 비밀의 행운 부적이야."

그는 주머니에 손을 넣어 쪼글쪼글한 당근을 꺼냈습니다.

page 29

아서는 얼굴을 찡그렸습니다.

"이걸 사용하면 넌 놓칠 수가 없어." 버스터가 말했습니다. 그는 당근을 아서에게 건넸습니다.

"너 이거 정말 확실한 거야?" 아서가 물었습니다.

"100퍼센트 완전히 두 배로 확실히 보장해."

"알겠어." 아서가 말하며 그것을 주머니에 넣었습니다.

연습하는 동안에, 아서는 행운의 부적을 손가락으로 더듬었습니다. 하지만 어려운 공이 그에게 오지 않아서, 부적이 제대로 작용하고 있는지 확신할 수 없었습니다. 프랜신이 공을 치려고 나왔을 때, 그는 쭈그리고 앉아 준비했습니다.

프랜신은 다음 투구를 오른쪽 깊숙이 쳤습니다. 아서는 공이 가는 것을 전부 바라보며 뒤로 뛰었습니다.

"펜스를 봐!" 버스터가 소리 질렀습니다.

아서는 즉시 멈추고 위를 보았습니다. 공이 내려오고 있었습니다. 그는 그것을 잡기 위해 손을 뻗었습니다.

page 30

공은 그의 글러브에 닿았다가 튀어나가 펜스를 넘어갔습니다.

"홈런!" 프랜신이 베이스를 돌며 외쳤습니다.

아서는 얼굴을 찌푸렸습니다.

나중에, 아서는 당근을 버스터에게 돌려주었습니다.

"여기." 그가 말했습니다. "내 생각에 이거 고장 난 것 같아. 아니면 아마도 운이 다했거나."

그리고 그는 걸어가 버렸습니다.

버스터는 당근을 살펴보다가 어깨를 으쓱했습니다. 그는 한 입을 먹고 나머지를 주머니에 넣었습니다.

5장

page 31

연습 후에, 프렌스키 코치님은 팀을 슈가 볼로 데려갔습니다.

"너희들 모두 열심히 해왔다." 그가 말했습니다. "작은 보상을 받을 시간이야."

아서는 버스터 바로 뒤에서 마지막으로 들어갔습니다. 다른 아이들이 모두 행복하고 여유로울 수 있다는 것이 그에게는 매우 놀라웠습니다. 아이들 대부분은 경기장에서 그가 했던 것과 같은 실수를 했었습니다. 그런데 어째서인지 그 사실이 그들을 별로 괴롭히는 것 같지 않았습니다.

"훌륭한 연습은 아이스크림을 받을 만하지!" 코치님이 말했습니다. 그는 테이블 몇 개를 같이 붙일 수 있을지 확인하려고 갔습니다.

page 32

"너 준비됐니, 아서?" 프랜신이 물었습니다.

아서는 그녀를 조심스럽게 쳐다보았습니다. "무슨 말이야?"

"아이스크림콘은 다루기 까다로울 수 있잖니. 네가 조심하지 않으면, 너 그걸 떨어뜨릴지도 몰라."

많은 아이들이 웃었습니다.

"쟤 얘기 듣지 마, 아서." 버스터가 말했습니다. "너는 우리 모두와 마찬가지로 아이스크림을 받을 자격이 있어. 하지만 네가 원한다면, 내가 너를 위해 그걸 들어줄 수 있어."

"고맙다, 버스터." 아서가 말했습니다. "어쨌든 말이지."

그들의 주문이 다 끝나자, 모두들 앉았습니다. 아서, 프랜신, 버스터, 브레인, 그리고 빙키는 같은 테이블에 앉았습니다.

프랜신은 불평하느라 바빴습니다. "우리의 문제는 타격이야." 그녀가 말했습니다. "우리는 좋은 타격이 없어."

아서는 그날 2번 삼진을 당했습니다. 그는 너무 빨리 휘두른다고, 코치님이 그에게 말했었습니다.

page 33

"내 생각엔 우리는 꽤 괜찮아 보여." 버스터가 말했습니다.

프랜신이 웃었습니다. "네 시력으로는 말이지. 놀랍지도 않네."

"내 시력에는 아무 문제없어." 버스터가 말했습니다. "난 당근을 많이 먹는다고."

아서는 안경을 만지작거렸습니다. 가끔씩 공을 계속 지켜보는 것은 어려웠습니다.

"어떤 사람은," 빙키가 말했습니다. "공을 어떻게 멈춰야 하는지 배워야 해." 그는 가슴을 쳤습니다. "공을 글러브 안에 가지고 있지 못하더라도, 공을 앞에 두도록 해야 해."

아서는 다리를 내려다봤습니다. 공들은 다리 사이로 자주 지나갔었고, 다리는 마치 골대인 것처럼 느껴졌습니다.

"우리가 기초적인 것을 배우는 데 집중한다면," 브레인이 말했습니다. "우리가 이길 확률은 시간이 지나면서 높아질 거야."

"그렇겠지." 프랜신이 말했습니다. "하지만 지금 당장은 그리 좋아 보이지 않아."

page 34

"글쎄," 브레인이 말했습니다. "네가 편의 머리 위로 공을 던지는 것을 멈춘다면 도움이 되겠지."

"나 안 그랬어!" 프랜신이 말했습니다. "게다가 그녀가 너무 가까이 서 있었다고."

프렌스키 코치님이 탄산음료 두 병을 들고 테이블로 왔습니다.

"애들아!" 코치님이 얼굴을 찌푸리며 말했습니다. "난 그런 식으로 얘기하는 걸 듣고 싶지 않구나. 우리는 한 팀이야, 기억해?"

모두들 입을 닫았습니다.

프렌스키 코치님은 테이블을 살폈습니다. "아서는 어디 있지?" 그가 물었습니다.

"1초 전만 해도 여기 있었는데." 버스터가 말했습니다.

"아마 냅킨을 가지러 갔을 거예요." 빙키가 말했습니다.

"저기 봐!" 브레인이 말했습니다. 그는 창문 너머를 가리켰습니다.

아서는 슬그머니 길을 따라 움직이고 있었습니다. 아이스크림콘에서 떨어진 방울들이 그의 뒤를 따라가고 있었습니다.

page 36

"아무래도 말할 기분이 아닌가 봐요." 프랜신이 말했습니다.

"그런 것 같구나." 그녀의 아빠가 말했습니다. 하지만 그는 오랫동안 다시 생각하면서 거기에 서 있었습니다.

6장

page 37

저녁식사 때, 아서는 조용히 테이블에 앉아 있었습니다. 그는 햄버거도 거의 건드리지 않았습니다. 그는 별로 배고프지 않았습니다.

D.W.는 전혀 그렇지 않았습니다. 그녀의 햄버거는 반이나 없어졌고, 그녀는 통째로 익힌 옥수수를 우적거리며 먹어 치우고 있었습니다.

"네가 돌리는 방법을 선호한다는 것을 알겠구나." 아빠가 말했습니다.

D.W.는 어리둥절해 보였습니다. "그게 뭐예요?"

"네가 옥수수를 돌려서 먹는 거야. 그 다음에 조금 내리고 더 돌려서 먹는 거지."

page 38

D.W.는 멈추고 옥수수를 바라보았습니다. "그게 제일 좋은 방법이에요." 그녀가 말했습니다.

"그렇게 확신하지는 마." 엄마가 말했습니다. "어떤 사람들은 타자기 방법을 선호한단다. 한 줄을 다 먹고, 옥수수대를 조금 돌려서, 새로운 한 줄을 시작하는 거지."

D.W.는 어깨를 으쓱했습니다. "제 방법이 더 나아요." 그녀가 말했습니다.

"너한테는, 얘야." 엄마가 말했습니다.

"너는 어떻게 생각하니, 아서?" 리드 씨가 물었습니다.

"네?"

아서는 듣고 있지 않았었습니다.

"넌 어떤 방법으로 옥수수 먹는 걸 좋아하니?" 아빠가 물었습니다.

아서는 한숨 쉬었습니다. "어떤 방법이든 실수를 적게 하는 거요."

리드 씨는 어리둥절해 보였습니다. "네가 옥수수를 먹으면서 실수를 할 수 있을지 모르겠구나." 그가 말했습니다. "사실이야, 네가 여기저기에서 알맹이를 빠뜨릴 수는 있지만, 그게 정말 중요한지는 모르겠다."

page 39

"아서 오빠는 옥수수에 대해 얘기하고 있는 게 아니에요." D.W.가 말했습니다. "야구에 대해 얘기하고 있는 거예요."

"연습은 어떻게 되어가고 있니?" 엄마가 물었습니다.

"좋지 않아요." 아서가 말했습니다. "저는 머릿속으로는 어떻게 해야 하는지 알고 있어요. 하지만 내 몸이 항상 따라주지 않아요."

"그게 지극히 자연스러운 거란다." 리

드 씨가 말했습니다. "참을성을 가지렴, 아서. 넌 주의를 기울이고 있잖니. 그게 중요한 거란다. 야구는 집중이 99퍼센트야."

"가끔씩 다른 사람들이 내가 어떤 나쁜 일을 하는지 집중하는 것 같아요. 그래도 프렌스키 코치님은 아니에요. 코치님은 항상 격려해 주세요. 제가 잘 발전하고 있다고 말하셨어요."

"너는 어떤 포지션이 편하니?" 엄마가 물었습니다.

page 41

아서는 멈춰 생각했습니다. "전 잘 던질 수 있어요. 그리고 공이 제가 있는 쪽으로 맞아서 오면, 전 정확한 장소에 갈 수 있어요…"

"하지만 오빤 공을 잡을 수는 없지." D.W.가 말했습니다.

"D.W.!" 아빠가 말했습니다. "너 한마디만 더 하면 공보다 더한 것을 잡게 될 거다."

D.W.는 다시 옥수수를 먹기 시작했습니다.

아서는 접시를 쳐다보았습니다. "D.W.가 맞아요." 그가 말했습니다. "그게 다른 모두가 말하는 거예요."

"말도 안 돼." 리드 씨가 말했습니다. "난 네가 긍정적인 기여를 하고 있다고 확신한단다. 아마 지금도 그것에 대해서 이야기하고 있는 사람들이 있을 거야."

"정말 그렇게 생각하세요?"

리드 씨는 고개를 끄덕였습니다. "틀림없이. 그러니 얼른 다 먹어라. 야구 선수들은 힘이 필요해."

아서가 고개를 끄덕였습니다. 그들의 첫 경기가 다가오고 있었고, 그는 준비되어 있고 싶었습니다. 그는 옥수수를 양손으로 들었습니다. D.W.를 한번 바라보고, 그는 그것을 줄을 따라 먹기 시작했습니다.

7장

page 42

"이건 고통스러워." 프랜신이 말하고 있었습니다. 그녀는 머피와 거실에 앉아 있었습니다.

"뭐가 고통스러워?" 머피가 물었습니다. "아니야, 말하지 마. 그건 야구와 관련된 거겠지."

프랜신은 놀란 듯 보였습니다. "어떻게 알았어?" 그녀가 물었습니다.

"왜냐하면 그게 네가 최근에 얘기하는 전부이기 때문이지. 더블 플레이... 커트오프 하기... 홈 플레이트 지키기."

page 43

"뭐, 그건 중요하니까." 프랜신이 말했습니다.

머피는 하품했습니다. "나한테는 아니야. 네 팀이 좀 잘하기라도 하면 이해하겠어."

프랜신은 주먹으로 베개를 쳤습니다. "나한테 상기시키지 마. 버스터는 던질 줄 몰라. 브레인은 뭘 하든 너무 오래 걸려. 그리고 아서에 대해서는..." 그녀는 고개를 저었습니다.

"너 그를 승진시키거나 할 수는 없어?" 머피가 말했습니다. "회장이나 단장 같은 걸로? 그를 야구장에서 쫓아낼 수 있는 어떤 것이든 말이야. 우리 아빠는 회사에서 사람들이 명색뿐인 높은 자리에 앉게 되는 것에 대해 항상 이야기하셔."

프랜신은 그걸 생각해 보지 않았습니다. "효과가 있을지도 몰라. 우리가 아서에게 여러 가지 흥미로운 일들을 주는 거야. 그는 매우 바빠지겠지."

"걔한테 멋진 직함이랑 부가 혜택을 줘." 머피가 말했습니다. "알잖아, 무료 주차라든가 유급 휴가 같은 거. 우리 아빠는 그런 게 중요하다고 말해."

page 44

프랜신은 고개를 끄덕였습니다. "맞아, 맞아." 그녀가 말했습니다. "아서는 아마 그 모든 걸 좋아할 거야."

"아서가 뭘 좋아할 거라고?" 그녀의 아빠가 부엌에서 들어오며 말했습니다.

"우리는 그냥 팀에 대해 토론하고 있었어요, 아빠."

코치님은 미소 지었습니다. "우리 팀은 잘 협력하고 있어." 그가 말했습니다. "물론 여전히 결함이 조금 있지. 하지만 그건 지극히 정상적인 거야."

프랜신은 그에게 미소 지었습니다. "결함에 대해 말이 나왔으니까 말인데요, 아빠, 머피가 아서를 경기장 밖으로 보낼 방법을 제안했어요. 그를 보조 코치로 승진시키는 거예요."

"오, 정말?" 프랜스키 씨가 물었습니다.

프랜신은 손가락 깍지를 꼈습니다. "어때요, 아빠? 제발요! 아서가 다음에 어떤 멍청한 짓을 할까 걱정돼서 공을 똑바로 던질 수조차 없어요."

"그거 참 심각하구나." 그녀의 아빠가 말했습니다. "너 아서에 대해 걱정하는 거지, 맞지?"

page 46

"오, 그럼요... 그러는 게 안 보이나요?"

그녀의 아빠는 턱 끝을 쓰다듬었습니다. "네가 걱정하는 것도 당연하다. 어쨌든, 그는 너의 가장 친한 친구 중 하나니까."

"그래서 그렇게 하실 거예요?"

그녀의 아빠는 잠시 동안 생각했습니다. "코치로서, 나는 모든 선수들의 요구 그 이상을 봐야 한단다. 나는 팀 전체를 고려해야 해."

"물론이죠." 프랜신이 말했습니다. "제 생각에 팀 전체가 이득을 볼 것 같아요."

"큰 그림을 보기 위해서는 훨씬 뒤로 물러서야만 한단다." 그녀의 아빠가 말했습니다. "나는 아마도 모든 것을 다 보지는 못하고 있었던 것 같구나. 고맙다, 프랜신."

"그래서 그를 승진시키실 거예요?"

그녀의 아빠는 고개를 저었습니다. "아니, 아니, 내게 더 좋은 생각이 있어."

"오?" 프랜신은 더 좋은 생각을 원하지 않았습니다. 그녀는 그녀의 생각 그대로가 좋았습니다.

page 47

그녀의 아빠는 턱 끝을 문질렀습니다. "맞아... 확실히 더 좋은 생각이야. 나는 아서를 승진시키지 않을 거야. 나는 대신 너를 승진시킬 거야."

"뭐라고요? 그러니까 저를 경기장 밖으로 보내겠다고요?"

"꼭 그런 것은 아니야." 그녀의 아빠가 활짝 웃으며 말했습니다. "나는 다른 승진을 생각하고 있단다."

프랜신은 그를 의심스럽게 보았습니다. 아빠가 그런 어조로 말할 때마다, 이상한 일이 반드시 생기곤 했습니다.

page 48

아서는 차고에 서서, 테니스 공을 벽에 대고 던지고 있었습니다.

바운스-바운스-캐치.

바운스-바운스-캐치.

야구 게임에서는 이걸 하지 않다니 아쉬워, 그는 생각했습니다.

"안녕, 아서."

프랜신이 진입로에 서 있었습니다.

아서는 그녀를 무시했습니다.

바운스-바운스-캐치.

바운스-바운스-캐치.

"이봐, 아서. 너 나를 평생 무시할 수는 없어."

page 49

아서는 공을 튀기는 것을 멈췄습니다. "무엇이 널 여기로 데려온 거니, 프랜신? 아니, 말하지 마. 내가 장담하건대 너 어제 이후로 새로운 모욕을 생각해낸 거야."

프랜신의 얼굴이 붉어졌습니다. "사실, 난 소식을 전하러 왔어. 우리 아빠가 나를 보조 코치로 임명했어."

"축하해. 비난을 책임지는 보조 코치로 임명된 거니?"

"아니, 아니... 있잖아, 아서, 내가 최근에 너무 열중했나봐. 미안해. 하지만 우리 아빠가 나한테 팀을 뭉치게 해야

한다고 하셨어."

그녀는 야구공을 꺼냈습니다.

"그리고 나의 첫 프로젝트는 너야."

"나?" 아서는 팔짱을 꼈습니다. "만약 내가 프로젝트가 되고 싶지 않다면?"

"너 그럼 항상 놀림당하고 창피하고 싶니?"

page 50

아서는 한숨 쉬었습니다. 그는 글러브를 들었고, 그들은 뒷마당으로 나갔습니다.

"준비됐어?" 프랜신이 말했습니다.

그녀는 공을 머리 위로 높이 던졌습니다.

아서는 그 아래에서 빙빙 돌았습니다. "내가 잡을게! 내가 잡을게!"

공은 5피트 뒤에 떨어졌습니다.

프랜신은 웃음을 억지로 삼켰습니다. "다시 해보자." 그녀가 말했습니다.

그녀는 공을 들어 공중에 던졌습니다.

아서가 글러브를 들어 올렸습니다.

"그거야." 프랜신이 말했습니다. "공 아래로 가!"

아서는 공의 방향을 따라갔습니다. 태양빛이 그를 앞이 보이지 않게 할 때까지 말이죠. 그는 팔을 들어 태양을 가렸습니다. 그리고 공이 그의 머리를 맞췄습니다.

"아야!"

"뭐," 프랜신이 말했습니다. "적어도

너는 공 아래에 있었어. 봐." 그녀는 다가와 그에게 보여 줬습니다. "글러브를 이용해서 태양빛이 눈에 들어오지 않도록 해. 그건 또한 글러브가 공을 잡기에 더 좋은 위치에 있게 해주지. 모든 것을 한 번에 하겠다고 생각하지 마. 단계로 나눠 봐."

page 51

"오." 아서가 말했습니다. "알겠어."

"한 번 더..."

그녀는 공을 다시 던졌습니다. 이번에 아서는 글러브를 태양을 가리는 데 썼습니다. 그는 돌고 돌았습니다. 그리고 공을 잡았습니다.

아서가 미소 지었습니다.

프랜신도 미소 지었습니다.

그들은 몇 번 더 연습했습니다.

"너 이제 요령을 알게 된 것 같아, 아서."

그도 그렇게 생각했습니다.

"고마워, 프랜신. 있잖아, 너 자신도 약간 조언을 얻으면 어떨까."

"나? 뭐에 대해서 말이야?"

"네 속구를 던지는 것에 대해서 말이야." 그는 쭈그리고 앉아 잡는 자세를 취했습니다. "자, 그걸 여기로 던져 봐."

page 53

프랜신은 공을 던졌습니다. 그것은 아서의 머리와, 팔의 개집과, 울타리를 넘어서 나아갔습니다.

프랜신이 공을 가지러 갔을 때, 아서는 멈춰 생각했습니다.

"좋아." 프랜신이 그녀의 자리로 돌아오며 말했습니다. "다시 해보자."

"잠시만 기다려." 아서가 말했습니다. "있잖아, 프랜신, 아마도 네가 나에게 공을 잡는 것에 대해서 생각해 보라고 했던 것과 같은 방식으로 너의 투구에 대해서 생각해 봐야 하지 않을까?"

"무슨 말이야?"

"단계로 나누는 거야. 봐, 네가 던질 때, 너는 다리를 먼저 떼고 어깨를 써야 해. 그리고 네가 공을 놓은 후에도, 너는 계속 그렇게 해야 해."

"어떻게 그렇게 잘 알아?"

아서는 조금 당황한 것처럼 보였습니다.

page 54

"응?"

"사실, D.W. 때문이야. 나 걔가 엄마한테 전부 다 설명하는 것을 들었어."

"너 지금 나한테 D.W.의 조언을 들으라고 말하고 있는 거야?"

아서가 어깨를 으쓱했습니다. "누구도 알 필요는 없지. 특히 D.W.는. 네가 잃을 게 뭐야?"

"알겠어." 프랜신이 말했습니다. 그녀는 준비됐습니다.

"다리... 어깨..."

그녀는 아서에게 공을 발사했습니다.

"아야!" 그가 외쳤습니다. 그는 글러브에서 손을 빼서 흔들었습니다. "그거 정말 빠른 공이었어."

프랜신은 기뻐 보였습니다. "그랬지, 안 그래?" 그녀가 말했습니다. "좋은 조언 고마워."

"천만에." 아서가 말했습니다.

프랜신은 잠시 멈췄습니다. "전에 너를 심하게 놀려서 정말 미안해."

아서는 고개를 끄덕였습니다. "뭐, 너가 가끔씩 정말 지나치게 하기는 해."

page 55

"내가 만약 또다시 너무 지나치게 하면, 나한테 말해줘. 약속?"

"약속."

"그래도 어느 정도는 네 잘못이었어."

"내 잘못?" 아서가 말했습니다. "어째서 그렇게 생각해?"

"뭐, 네가 공을 떨어뜨리지 않았다면, 난 너를 놀리지 않았을 거야."

"오, 정말? 뭐, 적어도 내가 공을 던지면, 그건 비슷한 근방에 떨어지기라도 하지."

프랜신은 대답하기 시작하다가, 갑자기 굳었습니다. 그리고 웃음을 터트렸습니다.

아서도 웃었습니다. "우리 또 그러네…" 그가 말했습니다.

9장

page 56

프렌스키 코치님은 벤치 앞에서 앞뒤로 왔다 갔다 했습니다. "좋아, 팀, 이게 우리의 첫 경기다. 펭귄스는 꽤 잘한다고 들었어." 그는 깊은 숨을 쉬었습니다. "하지만 난 너희들이 연습 때 한 것처럼 경기하길 바란다. 그냥 나가서 재미있게 하는 거야."

코치님은 손뼉을 쳤습니다. "좋아, 우리팀. 가자!"

이글스는 수비를 맡았습니다. 1회에, 공은 날카롭게 땅을 치고 아서에게 날아 왔습니다. 그는 정확하게 공을 잡고 2루로 던졌습니다.

page 57

"좋았어, 아서!" 버스터가 말했습니다.

그의 부모님들은 관중석에서 환호했습니다.

"저게 내 오빠예요." D.W.가 주위의 모두에게 말했습니다. "그가 아는 모든 것은 다 내가 가르친 거예요."

그 다음 4회는 빠르게 지나갔습니다. 각 팀은 2점을 올렸습니다. 5회 말, 아서는 두 번째로 타석에 올랐습니다. 이전 타석에서는 볼넷으로 걸어 나갔었습니다.

이제 그는 중앙으로 1루타를 쳤습니다.

"잘했어, 아서!" 프랜신이 벤치에서 소리 질렀습니다.

버스터가 다음이었습니다. 그는 두 투구를 파울 처리했지만 세 번째에는 크게 헛스윙을 했습니다.

"스트라이크 쓰리!" 심판이 외쳤습니다.

page 58

백스터 부인은 관중석에 서서 박수쳤습니다. "좋은 스윙이었어, 버스터!" 그녀는 외쳤습니다.

브레인이 마지막 두 회를 던졌습니다. 6회는 무득점이었지만, 7회 초, 펭귄스가 1점을 득점해 앞서 나갔습니다. 그리고, 원아웃인 상태에서, 5번째 타자가 안타를 쳐서 1루로 갔다가 오버스로로 3루까지 나갔습니다.

다음 타자가 나왔습니다.

브레인은 손가락을 핥아, 바람의 방향을 시험했습니다.

그리고 그는 홈 플레이트를 향해 던졌습니다.

따악!

그것은 높이 친 공이었습니다.

"네 몫이야, 아서." 프랜신이 2루에서 외쳤습니다.

page 60

"난 못 보겠어." 버스터가 외야 왼쪽에서 말했습니다.

아서는 잔디 위에서 뒷걸음질 쳤습니다. 그는 몇 번 눈을 깜박였지만, 절대 공에서 눈을 떼지 않았습니다. 프랜신이 말한 것을 기억해, 그는 자신에게 말했습니다. 그는 글러브로 눈을 보호했습니다.

아서가 펜스에 닿았습니다. 공은 빠르게 아래로 떨어졌습니다.

터억.

아서가 잡았습니다.

"전달해!" 프랜신이 소리쳤습니다.

아서는 공을 던졌습니다. 프랜신이 잡아서 빙글 돌았습니다. 주자는 3루에서 태그 업한 후 홈 플레이트로 향하고 있었습니다.

빙키가 기다리고 있었습니다.

"던져!" 그가 외쳤습니다.

page 61

프랜신은 투수를 하고 있지 않았지만, 그녀는 완벽한 빠른 공을 던져야 한다는 것을 알았습니다. 그녀는 발을 단단히 놓고 그에게 발사했습니다.

주자가 미끄러져 들어왔습니다. 빙키는 재빨리 그를 태그했습니다.

"아웃!" 심판이 외쳤습니다.

아서의 팀은 경기장에서 종종걸음으로 걸어 나왔습니다. 그들은 한 점 뒤져 있었지만, 여전히 마지막 공격 기회가 있었습니다.

게임은 아직 끝나지 않았습니다.

10장

page 62

벤치에 있는 모두가 경기장을 바라보고 있었습니다.

수 엘렌이 먼저 나왔습니다. 첫 투구는 볼이었습니다.

"좋은 공을 기다려!" 프랜신이 소리질렀습니다.

수 엘렌은 끄덕였습니다. 그녀는 타석으로 돌아갔습니다.

공이 들어왔습니다.

수 엘렌은 힘껏 휘둘렀습니다. 그리고 공을 왼쪽으로 선을 그리며 날려 보냈습니다.

page 63

프렌스키 코치님이 휘파람을 불었습니다. "좋아! 동점 주자가 1루에 있어."

펀이 다음 타자였습니다. 그녀는 힘없는 플라이 볼을 오른쪽으로 쳐서 아웃되고, 수 엘렌을 2루로 보냈습니다.

"계속 그렇게 해." 코치님이 말했습니다.

이제 빙키가 홈 플레이트에 섰습니다. 그는 운동화에 묻은 흙을 두드리고 야구 방망이를 위로 들었습니다.

공이 들어왔습니다.

빙키는 힘껏 휘둘렀지만, 조금 빨랐습니다. 공은 외야 오른쪽으로 깊이 날아갔지만, 펜스로 가기 전에 잡혔습니다. 그는 아웃이었지만, 수 엘렌은 2루에서

태그 업을 한 후 3루로 달려갔습니다.

버스터가 다음이었습니다.

"그냥 잘 갖다 대기만 해." 코치님이 말했습니다. "1루타면 동점이야. 우리가 살아서 계속 공격하게 해줘."

버스터는 고개를 끄덕였습니다.

그는 처음 두 번의 투구가 지나가는 것을 지켜보고 있었습니다. 원볼 그리고 원 스트라이크.

page 64

세 번째 투구가 왔습니다. 버스터는 달려들었습니다.

공은 1마일 높이로 튀어 올라갔습니다. 모두들 위를 올려다봤습니다.

투수가 잡겠다고 외쳤습니다.

아서는 숨을 죽였습니다. 아마도 투수가 잔디에 걸려서 넘어지거나, 태양에 눈이 보이지 않게 되던가, 갑자기 등이 가려워져서 글러브로 긁을지도 모릅니다.

탁!

공이 잡혔습니다. 게임이 끝났습니다. 펭귄스가 이긴 것이었습니다.

다른 팀이 경기장에서 달려 나오며 승리의 환호성을 지를 때, 버스터는 터덜터덜 선수 대기석으로 걸어왔습니다.

"애썼어, 버스터." 코치님이 말했습니다. "방금 그건 펜스로 갈 줄 알았단다."

page 65

"나도 그랬어." 아서가 말했습니다. "좋은 시도였어."

프랜신이 버스터에게로 뛰쳐나왔습니다. "이런, 버스터, 우리가 필요한 건 그냥 안타 하나뿐이었는데, 넌 그것도 못—"

아서가 헛기침했습니다.

프랜신이 그를 보았습니다. "—넌 그것보다 더 잘할 수는 없었어. 잘했어."

그녀는 버스터의 어깨를 토닥였습니다.

모두 집으로 향하기 전에, 그들의 가족들은 잠시 동안 함께 모였습니다.

아서, 프랜신, 그리고 버스터가 가장 마지막에 떠나는 사람들이었습니다. 그들은 마음속으로 경기 전체를 다시 그렸습니다.

"우리 정말 잘했어." 아서가 말했습니다. "그리고 시즌은 이제 시작이야."

"맞아." 프랜신이 말했습니다. "다음 경기는 더 나을 거야."

page 67

버스터가 어깨를 으쓱했습니다. "나도 그러길 바라." 그가 말했습니다.

"있잖아, 버스터." 아서가 말했습니다. "프랜신이 지난번에 나에게 야구에 대한 조언을 해줬어. 아마도 그녀가 너한테도 똑같이 해줄 수 있을 거야."

"글쎄..." 버스터가 말했습니다.

"그냥 네가 버스터 볼에 쏟는 모든 힘을 생각해 봐." 프랜신이 말했습니다.

버스터는 밝아졌습니다.

"우리는 단지 그 힘을 너의 야구 방망이로 보낼 방법만 찾으면 돼. 우리 언제 같이 모여서—"

"지금은 어때?" 버스터가 물었습니다.

"지금?" 프랜신은 주위를 둘러봤습니다. 경기장은 비어 있었습니다.

버스터는 야구 방망이를 들고 홈플레이트로 갔습니다. "자, 어서, 뭘 기다리는 거야?"

"아서?" 프랜신이 속삭였습니다.

"응?"

"내가 너를 놀린 것처럼 버스터를 놀리기 전에 나를 멈춰줘서 고마워."

page 68

"천만에. 그리고 나를 경기에 관해서 도와줘서 고마워. 봤지? 팀워크가 답이었어."

프랜신이 고개를 끄덕였습니다. "맞아. 그런데 말이야, 축구 시즌이 다가오고 있어. 그리고 네가 축구를 못한다면, 난 처음부터 다시 너를 놀릴 거야."

그러고는, 그녀는 아서를 홈 플레이트에 남겨둔 채 투수 마운드로 갔습니다.

"좋아, 버스터, 집중해. 우리가 처음으로 할 일은..."

아서는 미소 지었습니다. 그는 프랜신이 절대 배우지 못할 거라고 말하진 않을 것입니다.

하지만 확실히 시간이 좀 걸리긴 할 것입니다.

Chapter 1

1. B Buster and Arthur were walking along the sidewalk with their baseball gloves. As they walked, they tossed a ball back and forth.

2. A "Did you learn a lot last year?" he asked. Buster laughed. "Did I? Let me show you. Run out for a long catch."

3. D The ball rolled down the roof and into the gutter. It shot out the bottom of the downspout, passed between Arthur's legs, and rolled into a storm drain.

4. C "No place to hide," Arthur repeated. "At the crack of the bat, the ball is headed your way. Everyone is staring, watching your every move." "My every move?" said Arthur. "Of course," said Buster. "And not just your teammates. The other team is watching, too. And the crowd in the stands. Especially your family."

5. B *Exciting* wasn't actually the word he had in mind. . . . Arthur swallowed. "You feel the heat?" "Well, maybe not," Buster admitted. "But it's a tense moment." "Because everyone is watching."

Chapter 2

1. A At the ball field, a bunch of kids were huddled around the bulletin board, looking at the team rosters.

2. C "I'm glad everyone could be here for our first practice," said the coach. "As most of you know, I'm Oliver Frensky, Francine's dad."

3. B "Now, our motto is going to be 'Teamwork!'" the coach went on. "If you have a favorite position, you can start with that. But you'll all be moving around. Who's going to be our first pitcher?"

4. C "Excellent. We have a whole staff. Buster, why don't you go first?"

5. D "Almost!" said the coach. "Arthur, that was a very graceful leap."

Chapter 3

1. D "Well, there was a force on at second, so I took off the glove and threw it to the shortstop, who was covering the bag."

2. **B** "He said I was ingenious. Very creative. He uses words like that a lot when I make a play."

3. **C** "Yes, well, most of them played last year, and you didn't. Having a head start makes a difference. I had kind of the same thing happen to me."

4. **B** "It was when I first got interested in cooking. Of course, I didn't know I would end up as a caterer. I just liked experimenting with food."

5. **D** "Exactly. But I never tried to pretend I knew what I was doing again. And you shouldn't, either. Don't be afraid to ask for help or advice. You'll catch up soon enough."

Chapter 4

1. **D** "That's very nice to hear. I was just wondering . . . Is the ball very hard?" "Well, no harder than any baseball." "I see. I've just been wondering . . . What if it hits Buster?"

2. **C** "Stay out of this, Arthur," said Francine. "You need to concentrate all your attention on holding on to the ball."

3. **B** "You know what you need, Arthur?" said Buster. "My never-fail, always succeeds, one-hundred-percent guaranteed, secret good-luck charm." He reached into his pocket and produced a shriveled carrot.

4. **C** Arthur stopped short and looked up. The ball was coming down. He reached out to catch it. The ball bounced off his glove and went over the fence.

5. **A** Later, Arthur returned the carrot to Buster. "Here," he said. "I think it's broken. Or maybe it's run out of luck."

Chapter 5

1. **B** Arthur was the last in, just behind Buster. It was amazing to him that everyone else could be so happy and relaxed. Most of the kids had made the same kind of mistakes on the field that he had. Somehow it didn't seem to bother them so much.

2. **C** "A great practice deserves ice cream!" said the coach. He went off to see

about getting some tables pushed together.

3. A "An ice cream cone can be tricky. If you're not careful, you might drop it."
A lot of the kids laughed.

4. D "There's nothing wrong with my eyesight," said Buster. "I eat plenty of
carrots."

5. C "I guess he wasn't in the mood for talk," said Francine. "I guess not," said
her father. But he stood there thinking it over for a long time.

Chapter 6

1. A "It's when you roll your corn around before moving it down a little and
rolling it some more."

2. D Arthur sighed. "Whichever way you make the fewest mistakes."

3. B "How are your practices going?" asked his mother. "Not too well,"
said Arthur. "I know what to do in my head. But my body doesn't always go
along." "That's perfectly natural," said Mr. Read. "Be patient, Arthur. You're
paying attention, and that's what's important. Baseball is ninety-nine percent
concentration." "Sometimes it feels like everyone is concentrating on what a
bad job I'm doing. Not Coach Frensky, though. He's always encouraging. He
says I'm making good progress."

4. C "But you can't catch the ball," said D.W.

5. B Mr. Read nodded. "Absolutely. So you'd better eat up. Ballplayers need
their strength." Arthur nodded. With their first game coming up, he wanted
to be ready. He picked up his corn in both hands. With a look at D.W., he began
eating it across in rows.

Chapter 7

1. B "Because that's all you talk about lately. Double plays . . . making the
cutoff . . . guarding the plate."

2. B "Couldn't you promote him or something?" said Muffy. "Make him
president or general manager? Anything to get him off the field. My daddy's

always talking about people getting kicked upstairs in business."

3. D   Francine was nodding. "Yes, yes," she said. "Arthur would probably like all that."

4. C   Her father thought for a moment. "As coach, I have to look beyond any one player's needs. I have to consider the whole team."

5. D   Her father rubbed his chin. "Yes . . . definitely a better idea. I'm not going to promote Arthur. I'm going to promote you instead."

Chapter 8

1. B   Arthur stood in his garage, throwing a tennis ball against the wall.

2. A   "What brings you here, Francine? No, don't tell me. I'll bet you've thought up some new insults since yesterday."

3. C   "No, no . . . Look, Arthur, maybe I have gotten a little carried away lately. I'm sorry. But now my dad says I have to make sure the team works together." She took out a baseball. "And my first project is you."

4. C   "Use your glove to keep the sun out of your eyes. That also puts the glove in a better place to catch the ball. Don't think about doing everything at once. Break it into steps."

5. B   "How do you know so much about it?" Arthur looked a little embarrassed. "Well?" "Actually, it was D.W. I heard her explaining the whole thing to my mother."

Chapter 9

1. A   Coach Frensky paced back and forth in front of his bench. "Okay, team, this is our first game. The Penguins are pretty good, I hear."

2. B   "That's my brother," D.W. told everyone around her. "I taught him everything he knows."

3. D   "Strike three!" shouted the umpire. Mrs. Baxter stood up in the stands and clapped. "Way to swing, Buster!" she called out.

4. A   The Brain licked his finger, testing the wind direction. Then he threw to

the plate.

5. C Arthur reached the fence. The ball was coming down fast. *Plopp.* Arthur had caught it.

Chapter 10

1. B Sue Ellen swung hard—and lined the ball into left field. Coach Frensky whistled. "All right! The tieing run's on first."

2. C Binky swung hard, but a little early. The ball went deep to right field, but it was caught just before the fence. He was out, but Sue Ellen tagged up at second and ran to third.

3. B "Just make good contact," said the coach. "A single ties it. Keep us alive." Buster nodded.

4. A "What about now?" Buster asked. "Now?" Francine looked around. The field was empty. Buster grabbed a bat and went to home plate. "Come on, come on, what are you waiting for?"

5. D "Thanks for stopping me before I teased Buster the way I teased you."

Workbook text copyright © 2013 Longtail Books

아서,야구팀을 만들다!
(Arthur Makes the Team)

1판 1쇄 2013년 7월 8일
1판 10쇄 2020년 8월 7일

지은이 Marc Brown
기획 이수영
책임편집 차소향 김보경
콘텐츠제작및감수 롱테일북스 편집부
저작권 김보경
마케팅 김보미 정경훈

펴낸이 이수영
펴낸곳 (주)롱테일북스
출판등록 제2015-000191호
주소 04043 서울특별시 마포구 양화로12길 16-9(서교동) 북앤빌딩 3층
전자메일 helper@longtailbooks.co.kr
(학원 · 학교에서 본도서를 교재로 사용하길 원하시는 경우 전자메일로 문의주시면
자세한 안내를 받으실 수 있습니다.)

ISBN 978-89-5605-675-3 14740

롱테일북스는 (주)북하우스 퍼블리셔스의 계열사입니다.

이 도서의 국립중앙도서관 출판시도서목록(CIP)은 서지정보유통지원시스템 홈페이지(http://seoji.nl.go.kr)와
국가자료공동목록시스템(http://www.nl.go.kr/kolisnet)에서 이용하실 수 있습니다. (CIP 제어번호 : CIP 2013009575)